THE SOCIETY OF
CLASSICAL POETS

JOURNAL VIII

Mantyk · Phillips · Anderson · Grein · Magdalen

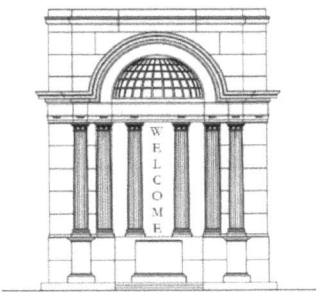

Rhetaskew Publishing

United States of America

Copyright © 2020
by The Society of Classical Poets, Inc
and Rhetaskew Publishing, LLC
All rights reserved.

All poets retain rights over their individual poems.

Editors: Evan Mantyk (lead), Connie Phillips (copyediting),
C.B. Anderson (selections), Dusty Grein (production), Daniel Magdalen (art)

All poems granted permission by poets and previously published on the Society of
Classical Poets' website (ClassicalPoets.org) between February 1, 2019,
and January 31, 2020

All contemporary artwork used with permission
of the artist. All other artwork in the public domain.

Cover Art Front: Eric Armusik, *Canto 4: Dante and Virgil Visit the Great Poets of Antiquity in Limbo*, 2017, oil on AlumaComp, 48 x 60 in. (EricArmusik.com)

Cover Art Back: Richard Samuel, *Portraits in the Characters of the Muses in the Temple of Apollo*, 1778, oil on canvas, 52 x 61 in.

"The Society of Classical Poets Edifice" on title page by Michael Curtis

Inquiries and Membership: submissions@classicalpoets.org

ISBN-13: 978-1-949398-32-8
ISBN-10: 1-949398-32-3

Contents

Introduction	5
I. In Admiration	11
II. Love Poems	85
III. Humor	107
IV. Exposing Communism	157
V. Pro-Life	173
VI. Observations	183
VII. Narratives	231
VIII. Translations	259
IX. Riddles and Square Poems	281
Riddle Answers	290
2019 Poetry Competition Winners	293
Poet Biographies	295

INTRODUCTION

by Evan Mantyk, President

On his way into the depths of the inferno, the fourteenth-century Italian poet Dante Alighieri, guided by the ancient Roman poet Virgil, sees a group of honorable-looking people illuminated in the distance. The two poets advance and come across a group of ancient poets: Homer, who is the Greek bard and father of all Western poets, as well as the Romans Horace, Ovid, and Lucan. They hold the most honorable position one can hope for in the inferno, or hell, where all else is dark. Pausing in his epic journey, Dante converses with the poets. What words pass between them exactly, Dante never says, but we are left to momentarily behold a scene of respite, of camaraderie, and of poetry.

This is the exquisite scene, from Dante's *Divine Comedy*, painted by American artist Eric Armusik as part of a project to paint forty large panels (each 4 feet by 5 feet) that display "the most comprehensive and realistic depiction" of Dante's *Inferno* to date. And this date—the year 2020—is of special significance since the *Divine Comedy* was completed exactly seven hundred years ago in 1320.

As classical poets, holding true to the traditions championed by the likes of Dante, Virgil, Homer, and others, we too find ourselves in a dark world, made so by ignorance that has led to systematic and sometimes vicious rejection of tradition. To give just one of too many examples, recently I decided to set up a poetry event at the Library of Congress in Washington, D.C., only to be told that formal poetry is "primarily visual." Confused, I asked the program specialist on the phone if we were talking about two different things. The poetry I was talking about, with meter and rhyme, is primarily auditory—a fact which is so obvious that the tone of the program specialist's voice disoriented me. I felt like I was walking into some kind of communist bureaucratic office during the Cold War and being authoritatively told that the sky is red, not blue (red, of course, being a more politically correct color in a communist nation). When I regained my senses and pressed the point, this person brought up the sestina and ghazal, both of which we almost never run in our publications and which constitute but a tiny speck in the vast history and world of classical poetry. I remained polite and the conversation ended. However, such is the muddled state of those wielding the most power in the poetry realm, or "po-biz" as Dr. Joseph S. Salemi aptly calls it, today. Given that, it is safe to say that the world we find ourselves in is indeed a dark world deprived of true wisdom's light, one like Dante's *Inferno*.

Yet, as in the painting, we are illuminated through classical poetry and find respite and camaraderie in it. As it relates back to the poem at hand, we see this demonstrated splendidly in British poet James Sale's 2019 book *Divine Comedies* and his *English Cantos,* which draw inspiration from Dante's epic poem. Sale's recovery from near fatal cancer becomes intertwined with Dante's journey. In his poem "Three Stars," Sale writes:

> We climbed from darkness far away,
> Opening ahead the circle round
> Through which we went from night to day;
> Yet strangely still they shone, profound,
> The stars forever and beyond
> Signposting our immortal way.

The stars that Sale draws on are a recurring image with which Dante closes all three sections (*Inferno, Purgatory,* and *Paradise*). Dante concludes the entire work with these four lines:

> Here vigor failed the tow'ring fantasy:
> But yet the will rolled onward, like a wheel
> In even motion, by the love impelled,
>
> That moves the sun in heaven and all the stars.
>
> (A l'alta fantasia qui mancò possa;
> ma già volgeva il mio disio e 'l velle,
> sì come rota ch'igualmente è mossa,
>
> l'amor che move il sole e l'altre stelle.)

Such poetry illuminates lives, bringing inspiration and hope to people of all backgrounds. Such is the beauty of classical poetry.

To conclude, in the spirit of poets' camaraderie, I offer my poetic translation of the "Preface to the Poems Composed at the Orchid Pavilion" (蘭亭集序; Lántíngjí Xu). The piece was written by Wang Xizhi (pronounced "She-jrr"), known as China's "Sage of Calligraphy," as an introduction to a set of poems created by a gathering of poets at the Orchid Pavilion in the fourth century—not unlike Dante's meeting of the great poets of antiquity. But here we find ourselves more in a heavenly setting, amidst winding streams and sublime mountains. There is also a light and beauty that touches everything, for the landscape is part of the poetry and all the words are recorded and laid bare.

At the Orchid Pavilion, the poets engage in a sort of drinking game in which poetry is spontaneously composed. Today, it is generally regarded as the greatest work of Chinese calligraphy. Although the "Preface" itself is not originally poetry, the Chinese language is especially poetic because of its repeated sounds, use of tones, and clear monosyllabic rhythm. This poetic translation has sought to capture the sense of poetry in the air at the gathering of literati that day and, in fact, on all days.

Preface to the Poems Composed at the Orchid Pavilion

by Wang Xizhi

It is the ninth year of Emperor Mu of the Jin Dynasty's reign, in the year of the Yin Water Ox, at the beginning of the third month (after April 20, A.D. 353). We are all gathered at the Orchid Pavilion in Shanyin County, Guiji Commandery, for the Spring Purification Festival.

> The noblemen arrive this day in Spring,
> From old to young, amidst these lofty mountains,
> Amidst luxuriant bamboos such days bring,
> Where spotless water gurgles by like fountains
> 'Round the pavilion and reflecting sun.
> The guests send wine cups floating down the stream,
> And when the nearest wine cup's floating's done,

INTRODUCTION - JOURNAL VIII

The guest must then compose and wine redeem.
Although we lack a minstrel's cheerful glow,
A cup of wine and poetry suffice
For letting conversation warmly flow.
Today the sky is bright; the air is nice.
A gentle breeze blows freely like our mirth.
When looking up, the universe is vast;
When looking down, abundance fills the earth,
Contentment greets the mind that wanders past
A host of sights and sounds of pure delight.
How wonderful to know joy's greatest height!

All men together live upon this earth,
And some of them will share their deepest dreams
In private with a friend who seems of worth,
While others recklessly pursue their schemes.
And yet whatever choice one makes in life,
Whether very sound or very rash,
When something happy happens, joy is rife—
But this, and youth too, lose to History's dash.
One becomes weary, losing heart, regretting;
The joy is gone as quickly as a blink,
A memory distant as a star that's setting.
All is ordained to turn to dust and sink.
It's been said, "Birth and death are both great days."
I sigh… How sadly on my mind this plays!

When thinking upon those who've come before me,
Their words and their regrets, I'm left
In sadness, though I know not why I should be.
Of course, I know life's gift is not death's theft—
To die when old is not like dying young.
And yet when future people think of me,
I'll be the same as those who Time's outrun.
How sad! And so, I've written faithfully
The names of those who're here, their poetry,
For even though the times and trends will change,

INTRODUCTION - JOURNAL VIII

What we regret remains eternally
The same, and you and I are not so strange.
For those who read our words in future years,
Perhaps, you too, will fight back swelling tears.

Illustration of Wang Xizhi from the book *Wan Hsiao Tang-Chu Chuang-Hua Chuan*, published in 1921.

I. IN ADMIRATION

Inseparables by Amaya Corbacho Martin, 2019,
oil on canvas, 33 x 40.5 in. (AmayaCorbacho.wordpress.com)

The Sound of Sunset

by James A. Tweedie

The gold-etched clouds of evensong intone
A whisper of rhapsodic melody;
Kaleidoscopic shards of psalmody
Aflame with facet-fire of precious stone.

The heavens declare God's glory from on high,
With anthems set ablaze by seraphim.
The music of the spheres resounds the theme
As day and night conspire to paint the sky.

Unshackled, unbound Beauty is set free
To wield a palette of cerise and rose.
Chromatic brush-stroked symphonies disclose
A sensuous foretaste of eternity.

As daylight fades and twilight colors dim
The stars awake to sing an evening hymn.

Previously published in *The Lyric*.

Glen Nevis

Lochaber, Scotland

by James A. Tweedie

Majestic, barren, rock-cropped braes ascend—
Arrayed, green-clad, in heather, gorse, and fern—
As mid-day, misty, dark'ning clouds descend
To cold-embrace each soaring tor and burn.

From heights unseen a torrent cascades free,
Unfettered into deep Ben Nevis' glen;
Then onwards towards Loch Linnhe and the sea,
Through sodden bog and brackened, stone-strewn fen.

Though hidden from the eyes of those below,
Ben Nevis' surly brow is sought and found
By those who brave the rain, the sleet, and snow,
To scale the cairn that marks its highest ground.

And there, amidst the cloud, God reaches down
To touch and bless fair Scotland's Highland crown.

BRAE: steep hillside
TOR: rocky peak
BURN: hillside stream

The Oban Piper

Argyll & Bute, Scotland

by James A. Tweedie

The sound was faint, and yet not far away;
A piper's chanter practicing a tune.
A youth, perhaps, rehearsing a new lay
At eventide beneath an Oban moon.

No thrum of drone, no windbag to inspire,
The piper skirled the haunting melody
With simple grace, consumed by Celtic fire.
I ken that he was piping it for me.

For somewhere deep within my soul I heard
An echo of forgotten memories—
Surprised, yet blessed, to find such passions stirred
By music carried on a Highland breeze.

The piper's tune remains with me today;
A gift he never knew he gave away.

LAY: song or melody
KEN: knew/know

IN ADMIRATION - JOURNAL VIII

Uragh Stone Circle

Count Kerry, Ireland

by James A. Tweedie

Beneath a weathered crag and barren hill—
Where mystic mist anoints the moorland rock
And whispered winds caress a heathered rill—
Encircled stones stand vigil o'er the lough.

As old as time, ere memory began
The rooted sentinels have stood erect
To mark the sacred place where mortal man
And nature's primal powers intersect.

A winter solstice dawn once brought forth prayer
And rhythmic chant to urge the earth towards spring.
Today, a flock of sheep has gathered there,
And bleating is the wordless hymn they sing.

Yet even here and now, as here and then,
The seen and unseen mingle in the glen.

RILL: small stream
LOUGH: loch or lake, pronounced "lahk"

The New Year

by Adam Sedia

The fields stretch out, bare, icy:
    Wide, blank, yet-unetched slates,
Tabulae rasae waiting
    The chisel of the Fates,

But deep beneath their starkness
    A mighty force has stirred,
The germ of the becoming,
    Unknown, unseen, unheard.

Its course is set in motion
    That none may stop or stall:
The seeds sown and forgotten
    Must sprout, bloom, fruit, and fall.

What shoots will break the furrows,
    Coaxed by the waxing sun?
What harvest will they proffer:
    When the sun's course has run?

For now they hold their secret;
    They tease the guessing eyes,
Which only gaze in wonder
    And fear at what shall rise.

TABULAE RASAE: clean slates

Midmorning Moon

by Adam Sedia

Translucent, pallid, gibbous ghost
    Suspended low to west,
Your splendor faded, washed away,
Drowned in beams of dawning day,
    Whose light you cannot best.

Alas! So lately you could boast
    A brilliance that outshone
The diamantine stars arrayed
Thronging through abyssal shade,
    Ruling night's realm alone.

Now overthrown, you wander, lost
    In empty turquoise breadth
Among the rose-tinged clouds of morn,
Dwindling as the day is born,
    Wasted to weird half-death.

And yet you course the sky: almost
    A specter, yet alive.
Just as to wax you first must wane,
When the sun falls from its reign
    Your brilliance shall revive.

IN ADMIRATION · JOURNAL VIII

Waves

by Adam Sedia

Turquoise waves on shell-white sand
Rush forth—crashing, crashing, crashing—
Dying gladly as they land,
Surging, breaking, foaming, splashing.

Lines advancing, rank on rank—
Never ceasing or deceasing—
On the anchored rock's long flank,
Neither tiring nor decreasing.

Soft, serene their rhythm sounds—
Slowly lulling, lulling, lulling—
Steady, steady, till it drowns
Every sound but inward mulling,

Awe at eons glimpsed as one,
Wave on wave on wave forever.
Can the world they overrun
Curb them? Never, never, never!

Previously published in *The Chained Muse*.

Speak, Thunder!

by Adam Sedia

Speak, Thunder! Let your booming voice resound
Out from the darkness of an angry sky
Across a land whose wealth of follies cry
For vengeance, whose unblushing sins abound.

Speak, Thunder! Let your intonations drown
The discord of our aimless chattering,
Our clash of tongues and steel, our blustering,
Our vaunted idols and their cheap renown.

Speak, Thunder! Let the fury of your rage
Lay low the soaring spires, the shining towers,
Level the walls that house the feckless powers,
And sweep away the clutter of the age.

Speak, Thunder! And the Earth, that seems so firm
Beneath our feet, down to its very core
Shall tremble, cowering before your roar,
A wretch, powerless but to whine and squirm.

Speak, Thunder! Thunder, speak the Heavens' thoughts,
Unleash the blasts of righteous rage withheld,
The floods that cleanse the nations of all blots.

Speak, Thunder! Thunder, speak the words of doom,
The words by which the wills of men are quelled,
The words that purify, but must consume.

The Architect

by Annabelle Fuller

He thinks in lines
And vexing vertices.
His shining mind always inclines
To math and magnitude, minute degrees
Of formulae, and the impossibilities
He has deciphered with those symbol-signs.

The architect
Perceives the things the rest
Of us forget. He can erect
The best and boldest buildings, which attest
That all the tensile, tractile talent he's possessed
Since childhood has allowed him to perfect

His mastery
Of masonry. Astute
Ideas spin out—the faster he
Conceives of his constructions, his acute
And obtuse rudiments, the sooner he can root
His schemes in pargeting and plastery,

In gypsum molds
Releasing casts which act
As replicas. Each model holds
The keys to understanding: what is lacked
And what's expendable's confirmed, and the exact
Proportions finalized. If he beholds

The opulence
Of Soufflot's Panthéon,
All marble-hemmed magnificence
Inspired by Greece and Rome—a paragon
Of peerless neoclassical finesse perched on
A crypt (Voltaire is interred there), immense

IN ADMIRATION - JOURNAL VIII

In scale and size—
He marvels at its sheer
Dimensions. Well-informed and wise,
His aptitude's unrivaled (his career
Relies on how his works objectively appear)
In every obscure, abstruse enterprise.

When he recalls
The cloistered colonnades,
The mansards, mezzanines, and malls,
The buttresses and boundless balustrades
Which won their ancient architects grand accolades,
Or how the Parthenon unfurls and sprawls,

Or how Labrouste,
Wren, Garnier, and Jones
Had calculated and deduced
The smartest, shrewdest ways to lay the stones
(In subtle, sandy, milky-coffee-tinted tones)
When paving the palazzos they produced,

He is inclined
To imitate their skills
And let the structures he's designed
Be panegyric odes to -burgs and -villes
And -boroughs that they built. He resolutely wills
His works to symmetry—walls all aligned

At intervals
Vitruvius advised.
With functions and reciprocals
He's shaping great Renaissance-authorized
Creations, like those Michelangelo apprised:
Vaults, viaducts, and voussoired vestibules.

IN ADMIRATION - JOURNAL VIII

His blueprint sheets
Use coses, sines, and tans:
The corner where each border meets
Is perfectly precise. His vision spans
From chart to site, inciting panoramic plans
Of grinning grids which lead to neat conceits

Like roomy domes
Which crown a fine façade;
Curved crescent rows of townhouse homes;
Prim promenades; a Paris boulevard;
Four paralleling porticos that shield and guard
A quad, like some concurrent palindrome;

Cathedral naves
Where glass-lit choirboys send
Out song, and incense wreathes in waves;
And mirrored silver-glimmer halls which rend
Each rapt reflection, making every shadow bend.
All these began as simple timber-staves.

He fashions dreams
With rafter batten-boards.
He gives them sturdiness, and seems
To realize fantasies. His art affords
Him awe, acclaim, well-paid commissions, and awards.
He made his own home's frame from diamond beams.

IN ADMIRATION - JOURNAL VIII

Castles in the Sky by Greg Olsen, 1991,
oil on canvas, 24 x 48 in. (GregOlsen.com)

The Dragonslayer

by Jeff Nicholson

Ere gloaming wanes, acceding sable night,
As writhen mists conceal a pallid moon,
From bastion vigil, thou descry a sight;
To rumors, foul and fey, thine ears attune.

Beyond the eaves of darkness lurks thy foe,
Where craven men are loath to tread—and lag,
Thou, heedless, don thy panoply and go
To mark the serpent's lair among the crags.

Ascending there, the beast, most wroth and fell,
Demands thou quail and abdicate to dread.
Instead, thou, wreathed in faith and trusting well,
Unsheathe thy sword and cleave the wyvern's head!

For God—thy fealty's charge—for love of men,
Thou liv'st each day to risk thine all again.

IN ADMIRATION - JOURNAL VIII

Sara's Prayer

by Joe Tessitore

Take me beyond all thought and word,
where only beauty can be heard.
Then silently, before Your throne,
I'll dance, Dear Lord, for You alone.

Claire

by Joe Tessitore

She dances like a flowing vine
that has the most exquisite line
drawn by the hand of the Divine
on this most grateful heart of mine.

POET'S NOTE: Sara and Claire are professional ballerinas and our adopted fairy granddaughters.

I Hear the Sparrows

by Joe Tessitore

No harvest moon, this morbid orb!
All that is warm, it does absorb
and now it eyes my frosty breath—
this pallid harbinger of death!

My frozen heart for summer grieves
as day breaks on dead winter leaves.
Their presence I cannot abide—
too long my patience they have tried!

These early shoots, well they portend!
This frigid grip is near its end
and none too soon; I scarce can wait—
for taste of June I salivate!

No measure for the joy they bring,
each time I hear the sparrows sing!

IN ADMIRATION - JOURNAL VIII

Refinement

Then he hid in the fire that refines them. —Dante, "Purgatory" XXVI, 148

by James Sale

We have seen threadbare souls, scarce out of hell:
One with a thousand sins stacked up against him,
But then one tear, one cry to Mary—well?
Then all is well; no descent, he can climb.

And as we weave the Mountain's side, ascend,
Dark circles recede, a-head's the promise—
So we toil, step by step, bend by bend,
Some fairer land for sure before us lies

Where every crime is canceled. Who'd believe?
And why? Don't we all feel it? Certain guilt,
For what we've done, do, further yet conceive?
But still these footsteps, one by one, still tilt

Inevitably towards that place where
The slime's all gone and, naked, we're before fire:
We tremble because we know God is near
And something too terrible to desire,

Although in one sense closer than our own self.
Stop! No further—but Daniel at that point smiled;
Something deeper preoccupied, something else,
And everything he'd known was less, was filed

Away, because only hidden in flame
Could justice that weighed stars be lit and shown.
There, mortal man at last might scorch his shame;
There, see God's point burning as if one's own.

Reprinted from *Divine Comedies*.

Mr. Adam Writes

by James Sale

I've had this cold six thousand years—
No antidote can cure its ill:
The sniveling, wheezing, coughing plight
That plagues the body till it's still.

I wish that I could find the pill
That stops the bloody mindless tear
That forms within the mind from sight,
And issues in a human care.

But it's too late; the quest is vain;
I'll never find the life I seek,
Or rid myself from living pain
Because the strength I have's too weak.

Only and lonely, dying's all:
But there—good God!—reversed the Fall.

Snapshot

by David Paul Behrens

The wind and balmy breeze
Blow softly through the trees.
All the darkness of the night,
Disappears in morning light.

The shadows on the ground,
Will never make a sound.
Birds awakened, singing sweet,
Make the forest seem complete.

This world we call the Earth,
Comes into view at birth,
For a brief moment in time,
In this universe sublime.

IN ADMIRATION - JOURNAL VIII

Bees Are Spectacular

by Leo Zoutewelle

When people talk of "bees" it well could mean
Two things: the sum of separate insects or
A colony—some workers and a queen—
A score of several thousand bees or more.

In some important ways they are the same:
Each single bee acts like its colony;
The colony fulfills each single aim
In pattern, preference, and prosody.

First off, note well, a strange and puzzling fact:
The bee is basally mysterious.
Its faculties in truth divinely packed—
Spectacular, and always serious.

A bee can mark a course like any plotter,
As much as three miles on a single forage.
While seeking pollen, nectar, also water;
They use a hexagonal comb for storage.

Bees are, as golden cooks of eminence,
Producing royal jelly, lovely honey.
As nurses they do work of excellence
In raising larvae, flying when it's sunny.

Bees' greatest attribute, perhaps, depends:
They can be sociable if treated well.
They learn to recognize those who are friends,
Then they will let you visit where they dwell.

That is to say, I think that bees have senses,
While "instinct" is a term used by the timid—
The ones who keep their thoughts behind defenses—
But bees have thoughts and use them to the limit.

The big point to be made, though, is the fact
That bees are needed to cross-pollinate
Our crops, to keep our food supply intact
So that our meal intake be adequate.

This is so meant to be a clarion call
That bees are just essential for us all.

A Treble's Song

by Leo Zoutewelle

Is there a thing to match a treble's song?
The joy perhaps of springtime larks in flight,
Or how the migrant birds so deftly throng?

What of the mane that speaks the lion's might?
The gentle rain that tempers summer's drought,
Or breeze to soothe its heat, however slight?

How could the essence of a basil sprout
Delight as much the tender means of smell?
Not very well—is there the slightest doubt?

Not so: a treble's voice will always tell
The vibrant heart: it does not take us long
To sing and reach the realm where angels dwell.

An English Ode

by William Glyn-Jones

That famous field where nodding poppies sway
In sunlit grass, where souls of all the good
Spend sweet Eternity in dance and play
And with the gods, take Beauty as their food
    Upon the isle across the sea
    That circles all the mortal world
With misty waters like a castle moat—
    How like must that famed meadow be
    To these fair fields where late I've strolled
These hills and lanes, these woods, this very spot!

Was it vain pomp or blind naïveté
That made the folk of ancient Egypt style
Their image of divine Eternity
Upon their earthly land astride the Nile?
    Where they might hunt in starry creeks
    Beside the starry waterway
Or find in starry gardens sweet, cool shade?
    Or likewise made the clan of Greeks
    Use Grecian fields where grasses sway
As models for their paradisal glade?

But no, let neither supposition stand
I say, that it was rather that they paid
The greatest compliment to their dear land
When seeing Beauty there, "Divine!" they said
    And so to English Summer Time
    Such compliment I wish to pay
As will the praise of those old pagans match
    The heaven forming in my mind
    The isle to which I'll cross one day
Has village greens and homes with roofs of thatch.

Autumn Sonnet

by David Whippman

This season's colors will be brown and gold
Fading to sepia, like a photograph.
The leaves, still splendid, are already old,
Their richness is a kind of aftermath.

This, like all seasons, is a time of change.
The new awaits, the old must pass away.
But this is autumn's theme, however strange:
Beauty is interwoven with decay.

For trees, for people, autumn time arrives.
Nature or Man, this law affects us all;
We all must reach the autumn of our lives.
Cities and empires, like the leaves, must fall.

This is the tint of autumn, briefly there—
The shade between elation and despair.

Timeless

by Rod Walford

Today I strolled upon the shore
Where Grandad walked in days of yore;
Along its sandy, glossy sheen
Where once his imprint would have been.

And thereupon I did behold
'Twas here, when I was two years old
I dangled from his sturdy hands
In gleeful awe of foaming sands.

So timeless now, this scene appears
It's altered not these fifty years
Nor hundreds… thousands gone before
As restless wave greets silent shore.

Still endless rolling surf she brings
Now to my little son she sings.
I held him in her gentle lee,
The way my Grandad once held me.

As every wavelet's dying throes
Washed tiny grains between my toes
I thought perhaps that in his day
For every grain, a pebble lay.

Eroded now by sea and rock
And pendulum of tidal clock,
Its pulsing rhythm, all abounding
In softest kiss, or anger pounding.

I pondered what it all may mean;
Our ocean's mighty time machine.
Where pebbles, hardened flat or round,
By rolling surf to sand are ground.

From rock to stone to pebbled grain
To sand, and back to rock again…
As, in our turn, we surely must
Become as ashes… dust to dust.

Roots

by Ramón Rodriguez

Cradled in my country's corn-rich plains,
North of the river, good and fertile land,
There is a certain wood that, when it rains,
Exhales a breath of life not meant for man.

That wood has given mouth-to-mouth to me.

A certain path meanders through the trees,
Soliciting and shameless to withhold
Its intimacies, all its memories
That time has touched, and that, like me, grow old.

The secrets there are everything to me.

Then let us go, and quickly, past the fence
And find the ghosts that linger by that tree,
Sole witness in this trial of innocence
And somehow soul of all I long to be.

May these roots be sufficient unto me.

IN ADMIRATION - JOURNAL VIII

Portrait of Wolfgang Amadeus Mozart at the Age of 13 in Verona
by Saverio dalla Rosa, 1770, oil on canvas, 27.5 x 22.5 in.

Mozart in Heaven

by Conor Kelly

Who is that smiling cherub whose huge wings,
Open, extended, like a swan in flight,
Lifts him above the angels to a height
From which he conducts, for the King of Kings,
Great open-air orchestral happenings
And plays concerti to his soul's delight,
Nudging the brass to broadcast all their might,
Goading divertimenti from massed strings?
Mozart is playing cadenzas for God
On a heavenly harp. He plucks with some
Zest, some irredeemable human love,
At melodies that never merely plod.
Rousing the souls of saints, he has become
The kapellmeister to the choir above.

IN ADMIRATION - JOURNAL VIII

Sebastian

An ode to Johann Sebastian Bach (1685–1750)

Sebastian: from Greek "venerable"

by Theresa Rodriguez

I touch the pages of your music. Then
My thoughts transport to times and distant sounds
Where you once dwelt. I think of you and when
I do a flood comes up from me, abounds
An all-consuming longing, yearning, ache.
Somehow I seem to feel what you once felt
When I begin to play or listen. Joy
Combined with sorrow, something you did make
An art form, from the losses you were dealt,
And morphing into beauty. You employ

All techniques of the mind and ear and heart
And reach my own. And I respond in kind,
And want to create beauty, too. A part
Of me belongs to you, because I find
You draw me into truth, and there I stay.
In reciprocity I always aim
To offer back to you, and God, the best
That I can offer when I sing. Today
I offer up an ode of love, and frame
It by the words I write. For I am blessed,

So truly blessed, to know the forms
In which you wrote. To sing chorales, cantatas!
A motet, mass, or aria transforms
The mundane to sublime! A suite, toccatas!
A prelude, fugue, the passion of the Passions!

Magnificent Magnificat! Baroque
Complexity excites me to the core!
Concertos, and the Goldberg Variations!
The pain and truthful beauty! Come, evoke
The substance thus within me, this and more!

Your mastery of harmony, combining
Such frank, sweet melodies which touch the soul
With perfect counterpoint: thus intertwining
Of several, making many parts a whole.
For you know joy; exhilaration forms
The "happy Bach" who dances. Trumpets call
And organ-powers attest. But one can hear
The pains of loss and longing, for the storms
Of death did take ten children. We hear all;
In plaintive strings your sufferings appear.

Not only what is written on the pages
But what is at the top—for there you write
Initials, signifying for the ages
Jesu, Juva, "Jesus, aid." And right
Below, the ending written, "S.D.G.",
For *Soli Deo Gloria:* alone
To God be glory. Prayer in music cast, when
Your heart is on display for all to see.
And so I feel a part of you my own;
A touch of soul mate, friend, the great Sebastian.

Magicians of the Night

by Landon Porter

Amidst the dancing shadows gray,
That mark the change to dusk from day,
A mesmerizing love affair
Begins in summer's sultry air.

Cicadas call in voices shrill,
Mosquitos bite and spiders kill,
As June bugs fly into July,
The sun departs, the breezes die.

Before the stars emit their glow,
Their earthen kin announce the show.
Sparkling bright with noiseless wonder,
Flashes lightning without thunder.

Teasing foes, eluding capture,
Near at hand then gone in rapture.
The act is grand, our hearts delight,
Bravo! Magicians of the night.

Moth, Angel of the Night

by Michael Zhao, high school poet

Emerging from a rich cocoon,
you shed off your old husk—
with legs outstretched and wings unfurled,
you head out in the dusk.

O harbinger of sunsets—
O twilight angel true!
The time has come for you to fly
out in the midnight blue!

You flit around from here to there,
imbued with majesty.
Enjoying cool unfettered sky,
Enjoying life so free.

O spirit of the open—
O sailor of the night!
You travel through the great unknown
while reaching for the light!

The time has come to rest at last,
for nothing ever stays—
All wings must beat a final flap,
All legs must give away.

O treasure born of treasure—
O rainbow found at dark!
Although you only stayed so long,
our world has felt your mark.

Your dance of death has finished here,
and off you drift, so still.
But you have passed to many kin—
a dance of life, a will!

Song of the Crab Nebula

in celebration of 50 years after Apollo 11

by Daniel R. Leach

Long before the first eyes ever saw me
    Floating like a ghost upon the night,
Long before human minds even feebly
    Pierced beyond their dimly shrouded sight,
I was there, though clothed in different raiment,
    Blazing like your own, my brother sun,
Over unimagined reaches distant,
    When your infant world had just begun.

When your wise men looked upon the heavens,
    I was but another shadowy form,
That no one guessed was the same which legends
    Told of, dying in a fiery storm—
Filling all the sky with brilliant lightning,
    When a spiritual darkness covered earth,
That, though darkened minds saw only dying,
    Was the herald of my spirit's birth!

Then I grew into a form more subtle
    Than the human eye could ever see,
Veiled as in a diaphanous mantle,
    Taunting your mind to discover me—
For within, a heart lies deeply hidden,
    Beating with a silent pulse that sings,
Hurling unseen beams across Time's chasm,
    Like the thoughts that move all living things.

IN ADMIRATION - JOURNAL VIII

I was watching as your great explorers
    Ventured on your planetary seas,
And when bolder minds dared to discover
    Things beyond the senses' certainties,
Waiting as you grew into a being
    That could feel my coursing, thought-like beams,
And, then recognize their higher meaning
    In your growing universe of dreams.

As with sunlight, tiny atoms quicken,
    Into earth's vast, living harmony,
Endless, untold worlds of thought awaken
    When, at last, you grasp my mystery;
When the passion for those passing shadows,
    For the higher, unseen things, you feel,
My dark beauty will no more elude you,
    Haunting like a thing unknown, unreal.

You will someday reach beyond the limit
    Even of our galaxy's own shore,
Spreading thought like light into some dim-lit
    Cavern that invites you to explore—
Then you will remember what first called you
    To whatever heights your spirit leads,
And I will be smiling ever on you,
    When you bend the distant stars like reeds!

Previously published in *The Chained Muse*.

Of All God's Living Creatures

by Peter Hartley

Of all God's living creatures only we
With subtle artifice create our style
Of dress and image, and with painted smile
Construct the me we want the world to see.
Though what they are is all that they can be,
Would any beast consider it worthwhile,
Supposing he were able, to beguile
His kind with such conceit and vanity?

"I want no artful guise" says one, "I know
No other self but mine: I seldom speak,
Though proud am I, I have no need for show.
With each among my kind I am unique:
And never will, ordained before my birth,
My like be seen again upon this earth."

IN ADMIRATION - JOURNAL VIII

Le Lever (Getting Up) by William-Adolphe Bouguereau, 1865,
oil on canvas, 4.5 x 35 in.

IN ADMIRATION - JOURNAL VIII

Reinigeadal, Harris

by Peter Hartley

So many years ago it was, a child
Tramped up from East Loch Tarbert's rocky shore
Across the peat hags underneath the wild
And dismal sky that overhung the moor.

No road could lead him thence, a mere track
Between the heather clumps, it weaved its way
Through crumbling gneiss, the acid bister-black
And clotted earth its peaty overlay.

And though remote, a little school was there
Some three miles distant from the nearest road,
Too late, it closed before, as all elsewhere,
They reaped the blessings that a road bestowed.

For then across the open moor abloom
With gorse it ran, hard-core laid down and sealed,
A hostel, no plush inn for those for whom
Upon a whim the "Spartan" life appealed.

Their isolation over, though for some
The road had ended rather more than this;
Our senses sharpened in detachment from
The mass, so much in aggregate we miss.

Those few would say a price too much to pay,
Such highways to salvation they disdain,
Inured to penury and pain as they,
To constant mist and constant driving rain.

The hermit life can bring us some degree
Of inner peace with independence, hence,
Resourcefulness and self-sufficiency
With self-reliance and resilience.

IN ADMIRATION - JOURNAL VIII

We find out who we are and need to be
If we're alone or nearly on our own,
We learn to cope outside our colony
And how to live without a mobile phone.

How hard sometimes in such a hostile land,
No company, forsaken by our kind,
In storm-force wind and sleet, to understand
Just what is with intelligence designed?

And then we must believe this life to be
A proving ground, though still the Western Isles
With much that seems inimical, agree
They're happier than we despite their trials.

For they are closer to the land and sea,
Less trammeled by association with
Their fellow man's complexities, and free
To dwell on past times, ancestry, and myth.

To sense the land anew each day they touch
It with a stranger's hand, see with the eyes
Of children microcosms, letting such
Creations bring us wonder and surprise.

In minute intricacies we can find
Within a feather, leaf, or powdered wing
Of butterfly or moth the mastermind
Behind the life and soul of everything.

As children may with wonderment acquire
Of astronomical extremities
In counting grains of sand at Luskentyre
A tiny hint of their immensities.

And closer to the numinous are we
Atop a Harris hill than ever he

In any Harris kirk on bended knee
On any Sabbath day can ever be.

A dismal sky still overhangs the moor
Today where years ago it was that he
Tramped up from East Loch Tarbert's rocky shore
Across the peat hags from a cold gray sea.

Winter

by Peter Hartley

In winter clarity is best of all,
Cerulean-bright the sky or Wedgwood blue
Revealing frosted cobwebs in the dew.
The ice creeps slowly over all to sprawl
In sculpted drapes on frozen waterfall,
Shapes Michelangelo could no more hew
Than cast in bronze the churchyard's wizened yew
Or bring to life the sightless in their pall.
And in the shortest days our menfolk brawl,
For when the nights are long their tempers fray.
The women call for peace, their children bawl,
The old become more bitter by the day.
For young and old the days are bitter cold
And each cold night more bitter for the old.

A Life of Austerity

by Peter Hartley

My grandfather was always old. The more
I think of him the more I call to mind
He seldom left his kitchen. We would find
Him sitting in an upright chair, the door
Pine-paneled, high-ceiled, lino on the floor,
And he would sit there all day long behind
A newspaper. The place for me defined
Him like the horrors of the First World War.

You see it spoke of his austerity.
He dwelled, like all the old in reverie,
A lifetime in his prime. Sometimes he went
To sleep, his nightmares we could only guess.
Sometimes again we saw an immanent
Serenity, a twilight peacefulness.

Trotters and Tripe

by Peter Hartley

A man of simple needs he was and so
Indeed was he a man of simple taste.
He lived upon a spartan diet based
Upon pigs' trotters, tripe, and offal though
It did him little harm. I didn't know,
But now in retrospect, I should have placed
Him there on high among the gods. Shamefaced,
It's far too late to say I didn't know.

For nothing less than patriarch he was,
And of his wisdom we knew nothing for
We couldn't say we didn't know because
To ask would show we didn't know before.
Pigs' trotters, tripe, and offal he would chew
And that I think was all we ever knew.

Bunny

a Mother's Day poem

by Sally Cook

Indebted to a simple spark of life,
You missed your chance at Europe's wondrous door.
A conscientious mother and a wife,
You danced your dance upon an inland shore.

Your simple fabrics catch my memory.
Aprons and cotton stockings made a trail
To sheets that sailed before the maple tree,
And yet you chose a froth of pale blue veil

To haze your thoughts, and everything I knew
Concerning you, your dearest wishes, lay
Covered, as the nasturtium seeds you grew
Beside your step. And when you could not stay

The colors of your mornings stayed behind.
My heart will see them when my eyes are blind.

The Pregnant Woman

by Beverly Stock

The Pregnant Woman nests a baby seed
Who's ever pressing on her very core
While her body adapts to baby's needs
She's feeling aches she's never known before.

A *linea alba* marks a fibrous path,
A vertical white line on her flesh
Of God's exacting hemispherical math,
Where muscles and the forming child enmesh.

The Pregnant Woman cannot seem to sleep
She warns that moods are swinging, family beware
And in her waking hours, she tends to weep—
The Pregnant Woman needs some extra care.

Long labor pushes her past vertigo
Towards the deepest love she'll ever know.

A New Life

an English ode

by Dusty Grein

With the blending of two souls,
in a dance as old as time
a spark ignites, and a cell divides;
a baby—hers and mine.

Conceived in a moment of utter joy,
a new and shining life
begins to make its presence known
deep inside my wife.

Soon the little flutters start
as miniature muscles twitch;
the first kicks then are seen and felt
causing skin to stretch and itch.

The mystery is half the fun.
A girl? A boy? Who knows?
A healthy baby's all we want
and pray for as it grows.

Watching as her tummy swells
and trying out new names;
We await the arrival of a brand new life
(but not the labor pains!)

IN ADMIRATION - JOURNAL VIII

Safe and Warm

a kyrielle

by Dusty Grein

For forty years and more you've held my hand.
You've seen me fall, and always helped me stand;
there is no danger I'm afraid to face,
    when I am safe and warm in your embrace.

You've shared my name, my heart, my life, my bed;
you've shared the dreams I've had within my head.
I've always known, your charm and gentle grace
    have kept me safe and warm in your embrace.

We raised our kids, and helped raise their kids too;
been up and down, and back, a time or two.
I've never had to fear losing a race…
    they all end safe and warm in your embrace.

We've learned in life, there will be raging storms,
but rainbows, after clouds disperse, will form.
My harbor's always been here just in case,
    you need me, safe and warm in your embrace.

In sickness and in health you've stood by me,
together we have built a family.
Regret and doubt, you'll find there's not a trace,
    nor sadness, safe and warm in your embrace.

Our time together here now nears its end.
Try not to cry my love, my wife, my friend;
my faith has always had a steady base,
    you've held it safe and warm in your embrace.

The light is fading fast—it's time to go.
Never forget, I've always loved you so!
Kiss me. I must your lips one last time taste,
    lingering safe and warm in your embrace.

I'll be with you each night inside your dreams;
For Heaven is much closer than it seems.
Hold tight to me as I slip from this place,
    forever safe and warm in your embrace.

La Commedia dell'Arte

by Michael Coy

The art of comedy's a sacred thing,
as fresh and precious in its gift of bliss
as when a worshiped one's initial kiss
transports us first. Like Fragonard, we swing
to Lena Horne's delightful rites of spring
on wings of wonder. No analysis
can pull apart a pleasure pure as this.
We humans laugh as nightingales might sing.
We're told to think creators must be serious,
but humor's both unruly and imperious,
and ridicule's the boy-god's sharpest dart.
We laugh and learn, though lifeless lead-weights weary us,
for dreariness is deadly, deleterious:
thank heaven for the comedy of art.

Micaelis Me Fecit

by Michael Coy

There lies a town in northern Spain
(thank God it's little-known!)
where every chapel, church, and fane
is hewn from honey stone.

Nice chunky arches, columns too,
with barley-sugar twist:
and gargoyles, griffins, gremlins who
quite cordially coexist.

To stroll here is to turn, with love,
some bestiary's bold pages,
and marvel at the mindset of
those early Middle Ages.

Capricious carvings crowd one door,
coeval "carls" of Beckett:
and, scratched into one caricature,
Micaelis Me Fecit.

The mason sits in effigy,
a chisel in his hand.
He eyes us quite audaciously:
that look, we understand.

He doesn't care for Time or Fame,
or Wealth, or Noble Birth:
that "Michael Made Me," is his claim:
and Michael knows his worth.

Ode to Leonidas, King of Sparta

by Ian Williams

Stern Sire and Father of the ancient West!
Sacred, your primogeniture appears
before the pride of Xerxes' bloodied Best,
"Immortals" bowed before these few brave spears.
What fertile earth awaits the Asian horde?
What day is come, abroad the sun-sparked seas?
What fruits, this greatest labor in the north?
The oriental cliffs that shade you, lord,
Bound by the Pillars, Strong-Armed Hercules,
The southern reach of Greece shall bring them forth.

Grim Parent of Europa's golden fields!
Anon, the multitude of hellish slaves
yell murder, thrust and punch your steady shields!
But now, what refuge? No more! Hold the waves!
What hateful power does this darkness hold?
An age of servitude, a world of char?
Shall men be chained who reach to pierce the sky?
Be forward! Bloodless in the slaughter! Bold!
Divine, that Emperor in his chariot-car?
No more a god than we who, fearless, die!

Fierce Ancestor of symphonies and art!
You held the line. What cowards hate to stand
became your glory, for in death your part
is played: inspiring, by delay, the Land!
Who rises from abyss of boundless time?
Who forms from out this blood-blest fallen host?
Who but the glory of this morning's light?
They are your sons, all sturdy in their prime!
Composers, poets, architects! The boast
of your great fall illumines dying night.

The fire of occidental history,
ploughed, seeded, watered deep, inspired from love,
is born; aye, love for folk; and ev'n for me,
perhaps, unknown except to fates above.
When will you see, O Son of Lion-King?
When live aright? When conquer in defense?
When take your bride? When Love? When Birth?
Where lives your blood, there singers still may sing.
Where strives your line, there poets guard from hence!
Where death to self, the rule of all the Earth.

Three Hundred Spartans

by Sancia Milton, high school poet

In twilight's ash three hundred stars await
As blue-black thunder roars with battle drums,
Three hundred voices murmuring of fate,
As odds and armor stack in fearful sums.

Oh watch, my brother, watch your patient steel,
And wield it knowing valor keeps you strong,
And feel, my soldier, feel what all gods feel.
When future matters not, our fear is gone.

"Alala!" cry our men when arrows plunge,
When Hades reigns, when blood encrusts our hands.
"Alala," sing we still, and onwards lunge,
From blood-slick fields to jasmine-scented lands.

So pity not our long-dead bodies slain,
For what is life compared to timeless fame?

IN ADMIRATION - JOURNAL VIII

Rider with Birds and a Winged Figure, detail on an ancient Greek (Lakonian) black-figured kylix (drinking bowl), ca. 550–530 B.C.

The Journey Home

by C.B. Anderson

Enwrapped in flesh we come to earth,
Created in our Maker's image,
Where from the moment of our birth
We're parties to a mortal scrimmage.

Just where the days ahead will find us
Remains a shrouded mystery,
But voices in the night remind us,
Despite our checkered history,

That places long ago prepared
Await the pilgrims who've departed:
Accommodations from the Laird
Who rules the homeland whence we started.

LAIRD: Scottish word for lord

The Water of Life

by C.B. Anderson

To die
Of thirst
Is nigh
The worst

And saddest way
A life may end,
Since quickened clay
Cannot transcend

Its fundamental need
For fluid that's designed
To irrigate and feed
The body and the mind.

We've been assured our souls are safe
And everything we've counted dear
Continues. Though our shoes might chafe
As we fare forth to face our fear,

There is a well that never disappoints
The expectations which inform our toil
And tribulation. Saving grace anoints
Both saint and sinner with the selfsame oil.

Inner Sabbaths

by C.B. Anderson

The One from Whom no secrets can be kept,
Who knows each detail of forgotten dreams,
Watched over me benignly while I slept;
And He from Whom no end of blessings streams

Forgave me for a multitude of slights
And graver improprieties before
I even asked. He lets me sleep my nights
Away serenely, helping me restore

My better nature. Such a friend is rare,
A diamond in a coal-dust universe,
An entity exceedingly aware,
A golden coin inside an empty purse.

And having said that, I am at a loss
To know how I can possibly repay
Such loving kindness, other than to cross
My heart, get down upon my knees, and pray.

Our thankfulness has never been coerced,
And surely this has always been His plan:
To let us choose when we will slake our thirst.
The Sabbath, Jesus said, was made for man.

The Winter of Our Contentment

by C.B. Anderson

Without the winter there would be no spring,
No snowdrops, crocus, scilla, daffodils,
Or any other bulbs that need deep chills
To send up flowers. Almost anything

Would be preferred to missing these bright blooms,
And so it is, we dream the reindeer hoof
That damages the shingles of the roof,
While we light candles in our living rooms.

We shovel snow until our muscles ache,
We clothe ourselves in insulating layers
And send the snow-plow guys our heartfelt prayers,
So they can do their job, for heaven's sake.

Ensconced within our private domiciles,
We sing the old familiar Christmas carols,
While undergrads at school roll out the barrels
And miss the season's point by many miles.

Come Solstice, when the days begin to lengthen,
A light divine that came into the world
Is lauded too: God's perfect love unfurled,
A newborn child through Whom our hope shall strengthen.

And then long winter months that tax our breath
Give way to days when gardens come to flower,
Just as the Savior, in his darkest hour,
Forsaken and entombed, defeated death.

Wings

by C. David Hay

Oh, to catch the winds of flight
And soar where eagles go,
To leave the woes of troubled souls
Behind me far below.
I'd listen to the song of birds
And sail in endless flight,
Then chase the sun through cloudy paths
And play with stars at night.

The boundless heavens for my home,
The breeze to lift me high,
To rise above my mortal bonds
And never have to die;
Knowing I had found the way
To trails where angels trod,
And when my wings could fly no more—
I'd take the hand of God.

Country Lane

by C. David Hay

Give me a road away from the crowd,
Away from the noise and the race,
And let me wander the quiet trail
To a different time and place.

Where miles are measured in valleys,
And birches point the way
To somewhere we miss so dearly—
We call it yesterday.

All cares are soon forgotten
On the path of no intent;
The beauty of the countryside
Is surely heaven sent.

And when the journey's over,
The memories shall remain
Of daydream trips into the past
Found down a country lane.

My Little Man

by Randal A. Burd, Jr.

I held you in my heart before I knew
Those dimpled cheeks and beaming impish grin.
Once quite the helpless creature, then you grew
Into the little man you are. And when

You speak with a maturity unearned,
Intelligence beyond your fledgling years,
Amazing me each day with what you've learned,
Your childhood much too quickly disappears.

Soon time will take this little boy from me—
Replace this child I love now with a man.
Whatever you decide you want to be,
I hope that you will always understand:

I held you in my heart when you were small,
And time won't change my love for you at all.

First published in *Westward Quarterly*.

Wind and Vanity

after Ecclesiastes 1

by T.M. Moore

My name is Solomon, and you may know
me as the king of Israel, David's son,
a man of wisdom unsurpassed. And so

I was. And yet I write to you as one
emerging from some near-insanity
and folly. I have seen, beneath the sun—

where all is only matter, time, and free
will—that the best of man's intentions and
exertions are but pride and vanity.

What profit from his labors has a man
when all is said and done? What difference does
he make? What does he leave behind? How can

he hope to be remembered, though he was
intent on carving out a legacy?
The generations come and go, because

death comes to all; the hungry grave will be
our common fate. And yet, the earth abides.
The sun comes up each day perpetually;

and then it sets, returning like the tides,
to where it rises once again. The wind
blows to the south, then turns and harshly rides

up to the north. It travels without end
upon its moaning circuit. Likewise, all
the rivers flow down to the sea, and lend

their issue to its vast, dark depths. Withal,
the sea is never full; the rivers cease
not flowing, whether great or small,

but hasten to the sea again, release
their substance, and return. And what of man?
Do all his pondering and work increase

his understanding of this life? Or can
they show the meaning of existence? Do
they save us from this vanity we stand

in? Everything is full of labor. Who
can understand it? We can never see
enough, or hear enough, or ever do

enough to make sense of this life. Thus we
are never satisfied, and happiness
eludes us. What has been is what will be;

and what was done—though it confound, oppress,
deceive, or disappoint us—will be done
again, to our enjoyment or distress.

For there is nothing new beneath the sun,
within that wall constructed by the mind
of man apart from God. Can anyone

insist that anything is new? Or find
out something not already done or shown?
Since ancient times it has been there, behind

the veil of history, waiting to be known.
No one remembers former things; nor will
the future thank you for the seeds you've sown

beneath the sun. You may obsess until
you die about your legacy, but who
will care? Or who for you a tear will spill?

As king, and young, I knew not what to do
to rule my people well. And so I set
my heart to seek out matters wise and true,

to learn by wisdom all I could, and let
God's Word illuminate my way—to guide
my thinking and my plans. That is, I set

my mind to seek the truth of God, and side
with Him no matter what, to live under
the heavens, not the sun, and to abide

there in God's presence, filled with awe and wonder.
Indeed, this is a difficult affair.
But God has set us to it, lest we blunder

in all our folly, turn aside, and dare
the heavens to challenge our presumptive ways.
Now I have seen the works done everywhere

beneath the sun, the heights of pride, the maze
of self-deceit, and all the vanity
and lies by which men prosecute their days.

It is all folly. But we cannot see
the crooked path we walk, because it seems
straight to us. Straight, though, it will never be

while crookedness and lies define our schemes
and set our course. Beneath the sun, we feed
on wind, and all our fondest hopes and dreams

IN ADMIRATION - JOURNAL VIII

elude our grasp, and disappoint, and breed
despair and anger. What we lack, we can
not find; we fail to meet life's deepest need.

So I communed within my heart: "Can man
know wisdom, knowing folly? I have gained
much wisdom—knowledge, too—more wisdom than

all kings who in Jerusalem have reigned
before me. I have understood all learning!"
Along with this, then, I sought to be trained

in folly and in madness. For there were, burning
in me, strong desires and lusts, which proved to be
my ruin, nearly. All the while, my yearning

to gain more wisdom grew. I came to see
that this was merely grasping for relief
from folly, groping vainly to be free.

For in much wisdom, there is much of grief.
With knowledge, sorrows break in like a thief.

At Twilight

by Erin Jeon, high school poet

The sun sinks deep into the hill
Behind the town that perches still.
An amber fog prowls through the street
Of cobbled stone and stonewashed chill.

Dark navy night skies come compete
With primrose twilight in retreat.
The fog's her shroud, her wedding veil,
For wedding nightfall in defeat.

In darkness heaves a biting gale
With crackled verdure in its trail.
The wind exhales its acrid sigh
Of sodden pavement and cut shale.

A single couple hastens by.
The sound of coats is rough and dry.
Low breaths leave swirled twin orbs of gray
Before they fast dissolve and die.

The ashen shadows lengthen, fray,
And fade as they go on their way.
Just barely rings their lonely stride
Until their footfall falls away.

Then stillness fills the cracks outside.
Taut calm seeks corners to reside.
Immobile movement charges night
With static, silence amplified.

The world is swathed in black and white
And amber giving moonless light.
Cocooned in night, the town sleeps till
It resurrects when day alights.

Pietà

by Tonya McQuade

His lifeless body cradled in her arms,
She peers with eyes of sorrow at her son.
In Italy, a hundred times I saw
This image of Madonna, so undone.

Distraught, she wonders how it came to this;
How could his godly father let him die?
Examining his wounds, his body bruised,
She searches for a reason, questions why.

On painted wood and canvas, Mary cries;
In plaster, marble, stone, her son lies still;
On tapestries and vases, humbly veiled,
This piteous saint reflects upon God's will.

In some, our Savior wears his crown of thorns;
In others, there's a halo 'round his head.
With just a cloth to hide his naked frame,
It seems the end has come, the Lord is dead.

Dear Mary ponders all this in her heart,
Yet knows her son had said he'd rise again;
She holds out hope, her fiery faith still strong,
That all this served a purpose, souls to win.

All frozen in that moment, so bereft,
These Pietàs, with sorrow, weigh us down—
So woeful, tortured, downcast, and forlorn,
As blood drips from Christ's side and thorny crown.

If, seeing, viewers think this marked the end,
The last time that this mother saw her son,
It's clear the story's ending they've not heard:
That Jesus resurrected, victory won.
I'd love to see the look in Mary's eyes
When to his mother he again appeared—
The love, the joy, the peace she must have felt,
Replacing all she must, at times, have feared.

Most famous is the marble Pietà
That stands inside St. Peter's, bathed in light;
A youthful Mary, in a full gown draped,
Holds tenderly her son, cold, stony white.

Carved by the sculptor Michelangelo,
The statue helped to launch his bright career—
The tenderness he captured in her eyes,
The way they, real and natural, appear.

So many have portrayed the Pietà,
Some adding saints and patrons to the scene—
In frescoes and upon cathedral walls,
On ceilings, tiled floors, and painted screen.

Their many varied forms inspire awe,
From ancient times to this, our present day.
I'm happy that, while traveling, we saw
So many as we journeyed on our way.

After the Rain

by Jared Carter

After the rain, it's time to walk the field
again, near where the river bends. Each year
I come to look for what this place will yield—
lost things still rising here.

The farmer's plow turns over, without fail,
a crop of arrowheads, but where or why
they fall is hard to say. They seem, like hail,
dropped from an empty sky,

Yet for an hour or two, after the rain
has washed away the dusty afterbirth
of their return, a few will show up plain
on the reopened earth.

Still, even these are hard to see—
at first they look like any other stone.
The trick to finding them is not to be
too sure about what's known;

Conviction's liable to say straight off
this one's a leaf, or that one's merely clay,
and miss the point: after the rain, soft
furrows show one way

Across the field, but what is hidden here
requires a different view—the glance of one
not looking straight ahead, who in the clear
light of the morning sun

Simply keeps wandering across the rows,
letting his own perspective change.
After the rain, perhaps, something will show,
glittering and strange.

Healing

by Jared Carter

All it takes is time. A blister
    develops on
Your palm, corpuscles minister,
    and it is gone
Within the week. The earth itself
    regenerates,
And color springs from that deep shelf
    or barren waste
Come back to life. In this way each
    remembered face
Or wave approaching some far beach
    falls into place.

"Healing" reprinted from *Peacock Journal*.
"After the Rain" reprinted from *Darkened Room of Summer*.

The Human Skylight

by Satyananda Sarangi

The skylight lets the nascent streak
Of gold inside this darkened room;
Some wisp of scent invades therein,
A perfumed faith to counter gloom.

Those orbs of light cast patterns old,
Of perching birds, of twigs, of leaves;
Though most designs appear archaic,
Their lasting touch, my heart perceives.

However good, this inlet be,
The raindrops seep and all is moist;
The dampened wall in faded hues,
Derides the hopes from days rejoiced.

And like the skylights, human minds
Are windows, letting in the rays;
As fancied thoughts and futile ones
Exist on alternating days.

IN ADMIRATION - JOURNAL VIII

Mysterium Tremendum

by Peter Venable

I muse upon the sea's expanse
And soar into a troubled trance.
A distant storm front drowns the sun—
Light fades into oblivion.

I ponder well mortality,
Though far from storm's ferocity,
As dusk settles a resting gull
And low tide's tempo brings a lull.

I lie against a dune, look deep
At stars so wide, so far, so steep
With worlds that circle and revolve—
I feel my bookish mind dissolve.

Our solar home? A cobalt dot
In orbit 'round a blazing spot.
Between the stars, the coldest space
Fills me with dread and chills my face.

Submerged beneath colossal night,
I seem a ghost clothed in moonlight.
I am awestruck—a shooting star
Singes the night with scorching scar.

As stars waltz 'round in gay ballet,
My veiny hands, uplifted, pray.
Despite the timeless void and death,
The Spirit breathes in vital breath.

MYSTERIUM TREMENDUM: a central idea in
Rudolf Otto's *The Idea of the Holy*

IN ADMIRATION - JOURNAL VIII

The Beeches by Asher Brown Durand, 1845,
oil on canvas, 60.4 x 48.1 in.

An English Spring

May 2018

by Nathaniel Todd McKee

How pleasant to recall the light of spring,
Which with effulgence breaks the woodland morn,
As we through beech-clad glade walk marveling
At overlay of Bluebells gaily born.
We then trace mud-caked paths to yonder mead
To view the golden oilseed spanning wide,
And though a time or two a compass need,
We come content to where we both abide.
As time proceeds new seasons it contains:
The vibrant foliage thick in summer's sun,
The vivid leaves an autumn tree retains,
Then hoary-frosted bark, by winter won.
Yet still the spring should rest within the heart,
For in the spring all other things did start.

The Music of the Earth

by Martin Rizley

In walking home from church one winter's eve,
I paused to hear the echoes down the street;
The dead leaves rattled dryly on the branch
And scraped along the sidewalk at my feet.

But far beyond, another, sweeter sound
Ran deeply, like a river through my heart,
A sound that cannot ever be compared
To music born of human skill and art.

It echoed faintly in the evening wind,
And in the cries of children down the lane:
The mystic, minor music of the earth,
So peaceful, yet so poignant in its strain.

No other earthly blessing can compare,
Nor words convey the joy I felt to hear
The somber, searching voice of Father Earth
Lamenting low the twilight of the year.

The Call of the Bush

inspired by John Masefield's "Sea-Fever" (1902)

by David Watt

I will go down to the bush again, where the days hang crisp and clear,
And cicadas hum their sonorous song from places far and near;
Where cockatoos flash across the sky, screeching all the while,
And the creek below makes a silver show as it slithers past in style.

I will go down to the bush again, where the campfire burns at night,
And the stars compete with the fire's heat to decide who casts more light;
And the evening breeze bears the scent of leaves, as sweet as love's intent,
As it lulls to sleep with a charm complete, when the talk of day is spent.

I will go down to the bush again, whenever I feel the need;
For the call of the bush is a strong call, and a call that the heart must heed.
And while I'm there I'll quite forget my cares, and the flight of time;
Until, with a sense of deep regret, to the world above I climb.

In The Know

by David Watt

It's easy to look without seeing
The beauty of life all around;
When moments arisen to being
Deserve to stir feelings profound.
To all of God's work lies a reason,
And all we ought do is agree
That ours is a duty to ease in
To our heart those wonders we see.

So next time the day fades to shadow,
As nighttime by increment grows,
Take notice of stars newly sparkling;
How sunlight reluctantly goes;
Birds hurrying home through skies darkling—
All gifts free to those "in the know."

The Clockmaker

by Benjamin Daniel Lukey

When I was young, I'd disassemble clocks
So I could understand what made them go.
With tools in hand, and pieces in a box,
I'd wonder, and I'd look, and then I'd know.
But lacking tools to take myself apart,
I understand myself through what I'm told,
And one friend told me I am young at heart—
Another said my soul is very old.
If I can trust them both (I think I can),
Then I have been—repaired, or else restored.
Is it sometimes the lot of broken man
To go back to the workshop of the Lord?
    Some say that Great Clockmaker stands aloof,
    But I know otherwise—and I'm the proof!

My Daughter Sees a Starling on the Lawn

by Mark Anthony Signorelli

I thought to tell you how the bird was called,
What symbol circumscribed the creature's being;
Intending to give your mind a better hold
On the unsought resplendence it was seeing.
But having gestured towards an utterance,
I caught the purple wonder in your stare,
Reflecting an unreflective jubilance
Of which your thoughts could hardly be aware;
And lest too early knowledge should destroy
The primal reason pulsing through your frame,
I held my tongue, and left you to your joy,
Sufficient with the grace before the name.

II. LOVE POEMS

Into the Light by Herman Smorenburg, 2007, oil on wood,
27.5 x 19.7 in. (HermanSmorenburg.com)

Song of the Rose

by Joseph Charles MacKenzie

The rose awakens, ere the sky
Has wakened to the sun;
And we, my one true love and I,
Awaken with a tender sigh,
To love until the day has run
And all our pains are done.

We part the burdens of the breast,
The weight of passing cares,
And gather roses, take our rest,
And count the ways that we are blest,
Each offering the other's prayers,
In our old hymns and airs.

For, the sky looks down upon the rose,
The stars upon the sky, and God
On all things, and our hearts He knows,
And Fair Love's face will He disclose
To those, in silk or leather shod,
Who soar, or search, or plod.

Today the Wind

for Elizabeth

by Joseph Charles MacKenzie

Today the wind through winter's unclad bones
Drowns in its woeful howl my soul's discant;
Beyond, a distant hunter's oliphant
Salutes the dead beneath their frost-bound stones.

Today the wind sweet music's loss bemoans,
No more to laud, beneath this canopy
Of slate-gray clouds, thy beauty's panoply:
Boreas blows his low, hibernal drones.

Oh, be it given me to turn the groans
Of the expiring year to song, and grant
That thy fair radiance release my chant,
On love's warm wings, to heaven's starry zones!

The Higher Charms

for Elizabeth

by Joseph Charles MacKenzie

It was a dream, or so I thought,
The subtle fire behind thy look...
Rare the creature that ever caught
My fancy, save within a book,
And rarer still the lass who both
The inner and the outer eye
Could please so keenly by her troth,
And make me sigh.

"No dream!" the voice of all things real
Exclaimed, though not in words, to me.
"The hour has come to break the seal
Of one last scroll, obscure to thee,
The scroll of Highest Being whose charms
Ignite thy true love's beaming eye
That captivates, and then disarms,
To make thee sigh."

On looking up, at once I knew
Why some men faint and some men flee,
Why some fatigue the ocean blue
With wandering from sea to sea,
But why the best reel in the ropes
To moor their boat for love's bright eye,
And hang their honor, fortune, hopes,
Upon a sigh.

Love's Gift

for Elizabeth

by Joseph Charles MacKenzie

We twain look on each other to behold
The sacrifice of each in worldly death,
That Love alone inspire our souls with breath,
Beyond the setting of our suns of old.

Love's gift is blood. The thorn and not the rose
Gives royal weight to the perduring crown;
And yet, be it of straw or rag or down,
Love's pillow soothes the head of fortune's woes.

All pastimes waste, all fleeting pleasures cloy,
The land of desires lay bare and in ruin;
Its sky is a void no bird ever flew in,
Its happiness a counterfeit of joy.

Lift thy fair countenance to heaven's rain
Of benedictions falling from on high:
Love is the hierophant of earth and sky,
The minister of jubilance and pain.

Here is the gate. Here, take its golden key:
Love's secret garden blooms in every season,
Beyond the noise of argument and reason,
Receive its Sacrament on bended knee!

In the Silence of the Evening

by Roy E. Peterson

In the silence of the evening,
As the sunset is receding,
Nothing more that I am needing,
Than a memory that's creeping
Just before my mind is sleeping.
Paramour and so much more.
As the French say, "je t'adore."

Fond remembrance halfway dreaming,
Keeper of my dreams is weaving.
What is that I am conceiving?
Fields of lavender receiving?
Is that you, I am perceiving?
Are you waiting at my door?
Memory please show me more.

Fluid fountain languid flowing
In the courtyard flowers growing.
Gentle wind is softly blowing.
Birds are sleeping; no more crowing.
Weaver of my dreams is showing
Beauty I have seen before
Coming through my study door.

Suddenly, soft zithers zinging,
Tympanic bells lightly ringing,
Angel fills the room with singing,
Mesmerized I sit unblinking.
Can you guess what I am thinking?
May my love whom I adore
Be my love forevermore?

Comely, shapely, so appealing;
How dare I describe the feeling;
Fills the room from floor to ceiling;
Out of chair I now am kneeling;
Just a kiss and senses reeling.
Let me close the study door.
Stay with me forevermore.

But the night too soon was fleeting;
Came the sunrise with its greeting.
While my heart continued beating,
Fell back in my leather seating
As my vision was retreating.
Though the heavens I implore,
Empty study nothing more.

When by day the winds are wending,
And the temperature is bending
Downward in a spiral trending;
Sleet and snow and ice are pending;
As another eve's descending,
Guess what I am waiting for?
Just my love and nothing more.

1/12/2019

by Edward Hoke

O how I long to hold thee in my arms,
And taste again of nature's sweet reprieve,
To cast off masks, false affectations, charms;
To savor all I had before you leave.

For thee alone I lie awake at night,
Tortured by the memories unmade,
For that alone I scorn all other sight;
The world without thee makes me wish I stayed.

I talked to gods I don't believe exist,
Yet I cannot be helped by any priest,
On meager scraps of us must I subsist;
A hell for him who turned away a feast.

I made a bed in which I cannot sleep;
Thy ghost is lonesome company to keep.

Love's Bliss

by Gleb Zavlanov

The Moon, torn from the Sun, her only lover,
Rose, starry-eyed and weeping beams of light,
A mourning widow left to wisp and hover,
A torturously pitiable sight,
Wan from the strain of sobbing out her eyes,
Now crater-like and dark from sleepless grief,
Still hoping that the Sun may streak the skies
And give her bitter sorrows due relief.

The Sun, torn from the Moon, his pale beloved,
Rose, swelling hot with grievous, tortured wrath,
Destroying every farmer's yield and profit
And desiccating all before his path,
Reducing teeming seas to lifeless dunes,
Transforming streams to rugged, scraggly dust,
Enraged and fuming, yearning for the Moon's
Smooth balming kiss to sate his torrid lust.

But unbeknownst to them, Fate now began
Gyrating the entire universe
In favor of these two, armed with a plan
To reunite them both, his love with hers.
In short, they'll meld the shadows of their lips
Into an ardent, momentary kiss,
The meager fleetingness of one eclipse
All that they'll have to savor of love's bliss.

Reply

by Michael Curtis

"I don't know what to do." you said to me
The day before the day before you died,
And I replied, "I don't know what to do."
Your eyes looked on in fright… We both cried.

And I am crying yet with pen in hand,
Unknowing what is best to say to you
Who now is bravely gone away to where
I dare not go. My sweet: What should I do?

Tonight I seal away your little book
Of verse composed in love, in lust, in fun,
Upon occasion, in response, in jest
To make you smile and laugh. Now, it is done.
It is over, perhaps. Yet, who can say?
In heaven, might we kiss again, and play?

Republished from *Bee-Bee Verses.*

Sandprints

by Michael Curtis

Yes: Life is pleasure, life is grand,
    Life is sweet and fleeting;
Alike a stroll upon the sand,
    Alike a heart that's beating
In measured pace, step after step,
    In meter through our days,
We grow, we build, and then we ebb,
    And then we wash away.
The waves are but the tips of sea
    That glisten in the sun
To kiss the soles of you and me:
    All things in God are one.
And here, with stars and ocean deep,
    We each awake to sleep.

Morning

by Michael Curtis

Uneasy is the sleep of eyes awake
    and gray
When in the dream of life asleep
    to day
You hear but do not answer me.
    I say,
"Good morning." then you smile until you drift
    away.

"Sandprints" and "Morning" republished from *Bee-Bee Verses*.

One Last Candle

by Angel L. Villanueva

The angry storm approaches in the night,
Its curdling howl is heard for miles around.
The trees all flinch in fear of nature's smite,
Then cast their sobbing leaves upon the ground.

No soul dare venture out to face the storm,
For nature's wrath is not so lightly scorned.
The lights go out as winds in anger swarm;
The frightened city now lies unadorned.

Yet here I lie in rest with you, my love,
As candles lift the veil that darkness brings.
Securely sleeping like a peaceful dove,
Your arms around me are your regal wings.

I gaze at you when calm outside returns,
And kiss your face as one last candle burns.

A Time Beyond

by David Watt

When time has fled away, as it must do,
And tresses strand-by-strand amount to gray,
There will emerge, as sure as night from day,
A beauty redefined—yet no less true;

For though your steps assume a slower pace,
Each movement will effect a pleasure yet,
Precluding any semblance of a threat
That passing years may lead to loss of grace.

And waking in the autumn of your days,
Remember then, these words of honest praise:
"Unlike the sun, which lessens after noon,
The light you cast will ever be immune."

And in that moment, distant now from youth,
You'll know that Love spoke timeless words of truth.

Shaman of the Waves

    by Theresa Rodriguez

I am the raging tempest tossed
upon the fretful sea;
you are the calm and quiet gale
that steadies me.

And yet I am the raging sea
as well as all its roar;
and you are even, still, the sure
that calms the shore.

And I am blackened night as when
the ship has sunk away;
and then I see your light which shines
as if a day.

And in the dark and cold, alone
I cry for one to hear,
and then you come; you are the lifeboat
drawing near.

This vessel that you are is strong
to bear all my within,
for you receive the charge with grace
and take me in.

You tilt against the whirling swirl
and navigate the course
so far from tumult, where I dwell
with ever force.

Your shoulder is against the gale
and me against your chest,
and we against the hollow gray
I come to rest.

I find mercurial repose
upon a curious shore;
because you gently landed me,
I ask no more.

And so we are of polar force
that meets in synergy:
you are the shaman of the waves;
I am the sea.

A Spot in Time

by Theresa Rodriguez

It is a moment or a spot in time,
When time is quieted and put away;
A simple thing becoming the sublime,
Suspended and eternal in a day

And all around me just dissolves to naught;
I feel my world around me disappears;
It is just me before you—I am caught
Between my happiness and many fears.

You look at me as if you've known before
All that I am in heart and soul and mind,
Or wish to know them, here and now and more:
These gazes that reveal and seek entwined.

For then I look up and I realize
I get lost when I look into your eyes.

Song at Sunset

by Connie Phillips

The sun sets 'neath the mountain top:
   A golden orb that blinks
And just for seconds lights the sky
   Ablaze before it sinks.

I see the sunset in your eyes,
   Heart sinking in your breast...
And bend to give you one last kiss
   Before your final rest.

A lake just isn't deep enough
   To hold the floods of tears
That swell and swirl within my heart
   When I recall the years...

Those years and years—all of my life—
   When you were always there...
The laughter, love, and joy I felt
   In that brief time we shared.

Though we expect and plan to live
   A life that we design,
We've no control o'er anything—
   To fate we must resign.

But faith the sun will rise again
   Will keep my spirit strong,
And keep you always near to me
   In mem'ry and in song.

I know you rest eternally
   With God—where you belong.

On Seeing You upon Waking

by Martin Rizley

I woke this day from napping, and I saw you lying there,
Across the room, upon a couch, asleep without a care.
The golden beams of twilight streaming through the windowpane,
Shone wondrously upon you like a rainbow in the rain.

Through moving trees, the filtered sunlight fell upon your face
In such a way as to imbue your brow with heavenly grace,
Erasing every line that marked the passage of the years,
And bringing out your beauty in a way that drew forth tears

From my delighted eyes to have your charms to me thus shown,
Like some celestial vision sent to bless my eyes alone.
A soft, supernal glow suffused your flowing locks of hair,
And kissed the petals of your eyelids, closed as if in prayer.

The radiant beams of eventide that brushed your tender brow
Appeared to share the deep affection I feel even now
When I think of your loveliness, and in my thoughts draw near
To lovingly caress your face so treasured and so dear.

Thus did those beams appear to touch your visage, not with lust,
But with a holy love uniting reverent awe and trust,
As one might touch with love and awe an angel by the arm
Whom heaven had sent down to save a favored soul from harm.

With such a sense of loving awe and gratitude did I
Look spellbound on your face as I was privileged to espy
Your beauty in full blossom in the dying light of day—
A sight emblazoned in my heart, forever there to stay.

Soul Mate

an alexandroid

by C.B. Anderson

My thoughts of you shall last until
    my bones are laid
To rest on yonder verdant hill,
    above a glade
Where somber weeping willow trees
    have set the stage.
Aloft on heaven's billowed seas,
    beyond old age,
I'll think of you again, to dream
    about the times
We lingered near a chuckling stream
    and traded rhymes.

Through Thick and Thin

by C.B. Anderson

Like moths to flame, like leaves that seek the light,
Old lovers might be drawn to fervent quarrels.
If one's to blame, yet fails to make things right,
It's only from a fleeting lapse of morals.

There is no shame in giving up a fight
If all the claims and counterclaims seem equal,
And when a name is whispered in the night
Endearments thus expressed beget a sequel.

The will to frame discussions free from spite
Grows weaker as the bickering continues,
But Sir and Dame both know the chance is slight
That either one would thrive in other venues.

Pachelbel's Love Song

by Michael Charles Maibach

When we listen
To his sweet song,
Did he then know
It'd live this long?

A song that gives
To every age,
A timeless sense
Of history's page.

Reminding you,
Reminding me,
Love songs can last
Eternity.

From age-to-age
Repeating ways
Of loving one
Across our days.

We know it's true
When our hearts love.
We know for sure
There's God above.

For He must have
Placed in our time
Our love to meet
So hearts could chime.

Pachelbel's song—
His lasting gift,
To heal our wounds
And hearts uplift.

When one sweet day
You love one girl,
Then to her soft
This song unfurl.

So years will pass
In harmony
And growth, entwining
Her heart with thee.

For Elba

by Clinton Van Inman

Pale would be the water
    Reflecting only skies,
Gracing not the splendor
    Of your enchanting eyes.
Pale would be the moon
    That only marks its pace
And fails to see the boon
    Of your much fairer face.
Yet paler is the poet
    Whose words cannot express
One word that makes you know it:
    That you deserve no less.

Her Love for Him

by James A. Tweedie

My true love laughs, and angel choirs sing;
The mountains echo back his tuneful mirth
While Nature dances, heav'n in step with earth.
'Tis music to mine ear; mine heart takes wing!

Into my love's embrace I fly secure,
And tenderly he holds me in his arms
As if to shelter me from sin's alarms.
Like rooted rock his faithfulness is sure.

If I could sing, my song would rise on high
As counterpoint to laughter's melody.
My thanks and praise emblazoned in the sky
To God, who gave mine own true love to me.

And so, with heart and mind and strength and soul
I sing of thee, whose love has made me whole.

III. HUMOR

The Great Debate by Jacob A. Pfeiffer, 2019,
oil on panel, 8 x 10 in. (JacobAPfeiffer.com)

Love Song for a Grapefruit

by Anna J. Arredondo

Dear Grapefruit, I of late have been untrue,
Seduced by sweet confections of all sorts;
My tastebuds languish, and my girth reports
Unwanted gain from my neglect of you.
The cakes, the cookies left me dull and slow;
My sugar-ravaged tongue is all athirst.
Now I crawl back to you in clothes that burst,
As bursts my longing heart, I love you so.
Oh Grapefruit, Grapefruit—orb of glowing sun,
Object of my poor palate's deep desire,
Fair fueler of my metabolic fire—
I yearn to see your healing juices run.
    Sublime and heav'nly citrus of my soul,
    As I devour you, I again am whole.

Ultimatum

To My Friendly Neighbor Regarding His Overly Friendly Pet*

by Anna J. Arredondo

Dear neighbor, do you love your cat?
(I'm sure you *must*, they're *such* enchanters)
I've got a bag of poo (for you)
It left in all my planters.

My dreams in spring revolve around
My growing plants of many species,
And *don't* include, at every turn,
Unearthing feline feces.

I want to plan my garden out
(It's going to be magnificent)
And dig and sow in tidy rows—
Not sift the dirt for excrement.

Please keep your precious cat away,
For if I catch him in the act,
The act will be his final one;
You mark my words, now, that's a fact.

So buy your cat a litter box
And teach the pest to use it—
If he comes back to soil my soil,
I swear I'm gonna lose it!

---

*DISCLAIMER: No cats were harmed as a result of this poem.

Dandelions

by Anna J. Arredondo

Through much plowing and seeding
And a great deal of weeding,
   My neat garden's a sight to behold,
While my negligent neighbor
With not one scrap of labor
   Has produced an immense sea of gold.

Nature Calls

An Open Letter from a Homeowner to the Users of the Park Adjacent

by Anna J. Arredondo

Dear frolicking, carefree, park-frequenting youth,
Please desist from relieving yourselves on my tree.
Though I do sympathize with your plight (yes, in truth)—
The absence of bathrooms plus strong urge to pee—
When I visit my garden, be my stay long or brief,
I prefer floral fragrance and sweet scent of pine;
So the next time you must use a tree for relief,
Young men, I adjure you—let it not be mine!

Why Pterodactyls Make Great Pets

by Mark F. Stone

Choosing a pet can be vexing and yet
it's important to vet all the choices you've got.
If you're in search of a pet who will perch
on your silver white birch, it's the best of the lot.
Dactyls are clever as hunters and never
go hungry whenever they're ready to eat.
Not just a yard bird, the dactyl's a guard bird
and, as such, a hard bird for others to beat.
Its beak and claws will make trespassers pause
and give cat burglars cause to look elsewhere for loot.
Dactyls obey each command that you say.
Thus, it's rarely that they must be given the boot.
Next thing to do is decide whether you
are inclined to own two, since the choice may be hard.
Two pterodactyls (and I will be tactful)
would be quite impactful when cleaning the yard.
Dactyls like dating, the joys of relating.
It's alienating to live all alone.
Dactyls may mope if you force them to cope
with the loss of all hope for a love of their own.
Dactyl romance should be given a chance
so I'll offer my answer, precise and succinct.
Always buy two, otherwise it is you
who, without meaning to, help make dactyls extinct!

Fleas

with apologies to Joyce Kilmer

by Rob Crisell

I think that I shall never see
A creature horrid as a flea.

A flea who makes a little nest
Inside the fur of doggy's chest;

That treats us like a free buffet,
Sucks our blood, then jumps away;

A flea whose bites cause us to swear;
That spreads diseases everywhere;

Inside our skin its eggs have lain;
It seems to like inflicting pain.

I wish that God had checked with me
Before he chose to make a flea.

On the Untimely Demise of My Hair

by Rob Crisell

In days gone by when life for me looked bright,
And I rejoiced in the clear dawn of youth,
My hair filled my soul with such sweet delight
That soon my locks became my only truth.
Time hurried past as fast as a spring day,
And still I adored my elegant mane,
Until one night, to my utter dismay,
I saw my hairs clogging the shower drain.
Alarmed, I prayed: "Dear Lord, please save my mop
And I'll atone for my arrogant years."
Alas, my hair's retreat refused to stop,
In spite of the use of Rogaine and tears.
And now here I sit, as bald as a pear,
Writing a sonnet on losing my hair.

Freakish Tattooing

by Joseph S. Salemi

The world is filled with brainless brats
Who all insist on having tats.
These morons with their inked-up bods
Walk about like savage gods
Displaying, to the public's view,
A poisoned skin of garish hue.
Their ugliness defies belief—
Your mind's been shipwrecked on a reef
If you think tats are cool and cute.
You look just like some feral brute
Who lumbers through the vegetation
Of some far-off jungle nation,
Or some circus sideshow freak
As retch-inducing as a geek.
In the past, tattoos were sported
By lifetime sailors, or distorted
Characters like thieves and sluts,
Hit-men, thugs, and low-class mutts.
A decent guy just wouldn't do it,
Or did it once, and then would rue it.
Maybe some drunken night his pals
Assured him he'd impress the gals,
And after several belts of gin
They got him to entrust his skin
To one of the downtown seedy shops
Not yet shuttered by the cops.
Now he's stuck with it forever—
There's no way that the guy can sever
Stupid designs from off his arm;
He's marked like cattle on the farm.
And girls—you think you'll get a man
With a tramp-stamp on your can?

HUMOR - JOURNAL VIII

Or that a guy will marry you
If you're colored green and blue?
Why deface your perfect bod
With images bizarre and odd?
Wise up, ladies—don't go nuts.
Tattoos are the mark of sluts.
Inked-up jerks have all forgotten
That even well-toned flesh gets rotten.
Imagine when you're gray and old,
Your skin in shrunken, wrinkled rolls
All scaly with dermatic crud
And mottled by your sluggish blood.
What will your tats look like *then*?
You'll resemble what a fen
Gives up to those who dig with slanes
To harvest peat: the drenched remains
Of those who drowned in ages past
And are brought to sight at last
As horrid, blackened, grotesque stiffs
All giving off putrescent whiffs.
Is that what you hope to resemble?
A dinge-dark corpse that makes folk tremble?
Tattooing is obscene, so please—
Avoid it, as you would disease.

From *A Gallery of Ethopaths*.

The Collapse of Character

by Joseph S. Salemi

What generates the half-assed views
That this dimwit nation spews?
Why are persons mindless lemmings?
From what source is this stuff stemming?
Collapse of character's the cause:
A nation's strength lies not in laws
Or money, soldiers, guns, police—
These things just maintain the peace.
The iron in each person's spine
Keeps us stable and in line,
And if that iron's rusted out
The country won't survive a bout
Of warfare, trouble, bad luck, pain…
It can't face up to stress or strain.
An army of three score battalions,
Or booted cops on panting stallions,
Or gold bars stacked in Knox's vaults
Are useless against grave assaults
If citizens are swishy wimps
As boneless as a shoal of shrimps.
And that's what we've become today:
Narcissistic dorks at play,
Obsessed with "how we think and feel"
And lacking any moral steel.
You see this best in "victimhood"—
A posture that's now understood
To grant one privileges and rights
That trump all else. The smallest slights
Become a kind of tragic pain
That lawyers milk for easy gain.

HUMOR - JOURNAL VIII

A language I call "Victimese"
(As common now as cheddar cheese)
Is spoken by a million boobs
As mindless as dead TV tubes:
I've been wronged, demeaned, oppressed!
My urgent needs must be addressed!
Our age resounds in cliché prating
But of all whines, the one most grating
Comes from the self-styled bleeding "victim"
Who moans as if the world had picked him
Out for especial exploitation,
Torturing pain, and condemnation.
You see these victims everyplace
Posturing profile and full-face,
Telling how they received a blast
Of psychic trauma in their past
From evil fathers or weak mothers,
From overbearing elder brothers,
From cruel, unfeeling, hard-boiled teachers,
From straitlaced nuns or wicked preachers;
How race or gender or sex preference
Meant they got no share of deference;
How they were made to feel ashamed;
How they were mocked or teased or blamed;
How they were never praised or flattered.
As a result, their pride was shattered
And this abuse has left deep traces
Making them psychic basket cases
Who cannot function up to standard.
But they'll consider themselves slandered
If you concede your full assent
Saying you know just what they meant.
When next you meet these sorts of whiners
Just hit them with these quick one-liners:

HUMOR - JOURNAL VIII

"Yes, you're a poor neurotic cripple
Glued to some ethopathic nipple.
Sorry you're such a wiped-out loser:
A nerd or whore or idle schmoozer."
If you say this, they'll go berserk
And shout that you're a callous jerk
Whose outer shell's too rough and spiky
To rub on someone's wounded psyche.
They'll run to their support groups screaming
And see their therapists that evening.
Such nonsense is now commonplace—
There's no one left who has the grace
To keep pathology well hidden.
They open up to you, unbidden,
And tell you how screwed up they are,
Revealing every psychic scar,
Every flaw and moral failing,
Sicknesses from which they're ailing,
Or their traumatized persona
Canyon-gashed like Arizona.
This age abounds in infantilish
Twits who think dysfunction's stylish,
And they assume the world can't wait
To hear about their parlous state.

From *A Gallery of Ethopaths*.

Compulsive Euphemism

by Joseph S. Salemi

Ethopaths fear, as much as cancer,
A straight, unvarnished, simple answer.
They love the euphemistic chatter
That clouds up an essential matter.
Seeing things clearly and addressing
Their substance with no elaborate dressing
Strikes ethopaths as plain immoral.
They'd rather take a dose of chloral
Than state the facts in simple fashion.
In fact, they have an ingrained passion
For phrasing that obscures and covers,
And this is why their language suffers:
Circumlocution leads to blunder
That tears one's sound and sense asunder,
Or else makes speech as *gauche* and clunky
As that of a State Department flunky.
They talk of the *undeveloped nations*
When they mean wastes and desolations;
Putting taxpayers through the screws
Is called *enhancing revenues*;
They speak of an *out-of-wedlock* child
When bastard is how he should be styled.
They'll term the stride of Stephen Hawking
As *muscularly challenged walking*—
A euphemism most elastic:
Back in the past he was a spastic.
Having a cigarette and whiskey
Is *substance abuse*, and far too risky
To merit much more than stern rebuke.
Such prissiness can make one puke.
Sometimes they dress up outright lies
In an upscale and chic disguise

HUMOR - JOURNAL VIII

Meaning, when they say *World Opinion*,
The New York Times and its smug minyan
Of inbred editorial hacks
And pompous governmental flacks.
They clamor for language that's *inclusive*
When they mean censorship's intrusive
Finger in how you choose each pronoun.
It's hard to obtain the simple low-down
On just what an ethopath is saying.
His words are a kind of crypto-praying
Where discourse is like a charm or spell
Keeping one safe in a verbal shell
Away from the brutish world of fact,
Unmanageable save by discreet tact.
Besides such gaseous obfuscation
Ethopaths turn all conversation
Into a surreptitious pleading
For things that they think the world is needing.
Statements by ethopathic vermin
Always contain a coded sermon
Telling one how one ought to think.
Language for them is just a link
In their relentless urge to lecture,
And you can tell the verbal texture
Of every ethopathic speech—
They all advise, prescribe, and preach.
Old Petrarch said the eyes revealed
That which the soul would keep concealed.
With ethopaths, it's the wagging tongue
That shows the stuff from which they're spun.

From *A Gallery of Ethopaths*.

The Teacher to His Students

by David Galef

The traffic light turns green. Your car won't budge.
You're either texting or completely blind.
And when you do proceed, you're slow as fudge.
You're still engrossed. We've come to know your kind.

Or maybe you're just walking down the street.
The sidewalk's safe enough to use your phone,
And yet you can't pick up your own two feet.
Your conversation stops you still as stone.

In bathrooms, too: so damned oblivious,
To piss with one hand while still on your cell.
The flushing renders it invidious
And makes your private time a public hell.

Okay, it's an addiction—but your doom
If I spot busy thumbs in my classroom.

Blue's Didgeridoo

by David Watt

From the stations they sent out a call
To their jillaroo friends—one and all;
For an overnight camp, while the sky bore the stamp
Of a cloudless day darkened from view.

So they came in farm utes, with their dogs:
Kitted out in their boots, working togs;
And they lit a campfire, letting flickers inspire
Tales of station life—some of them true!

And the girls placed their boots in a pile
To relieve their tired toes for a while;
While each dog roamed about, and with curious snout
Found the mischief they thought was their due.

One young dog, name of "Blue," loved a game,
And that night his play led him to fame;
For he took every boot, without girl in pursuit,
And he stowed them where nobody knew;

And the place that he chose was a log,
Straight and hollow—just right for a dog
To deposit within, boots well-heeled, some worn thin,
Where the gaggle of girls had no clue!

When the jillaroos saw their demise
They could scarcely believe their own eyes!
Though they searched, shod in socks, under bushes and rocks,
Not a trace of their footwear showed through.

And in cattle-dog style, cunning "Blue"
Rested paws over ears, saw it through;
Until, tender of feet, they admitted defeat—
For there wasn't much else they could do!

And they say, when the wind blows just right,
Through that log on a Kimberley night;
Those elasticized sides, hidden safely inside,
Resonate like a didgeridoo.

JILLAROO: a young woman in training on a sheep or cattle farm
UTE: utility vehicle with a pickup tray at the rear
TOGS: clothing
KIMBERLEY: the sparsely settled Kimberley region of Western Australia
DIDGERIDOO: a wind instrument developed by indigenous Australians

Armilustrium

by Michael Curtis

I shall surely miss you, pretty flower:
O Gladius, you have been sweet to me.
Your shapely waist is comforting in lonely
Nights; in heat you show a lusty temper,
Always fierce, the first to thrust and slaughter.
I shall miss you, Gladius. My sweet-pea,
Scutum: It was you who kept me free
Of holes, of stabs, and slashes. Forever
Shall I be fond of you, my good Scutum.
Come! And let us step along with tubas,
Parade ourselves before the big Pooh-Bahs.
Then, we shall take a rest, a wash and groom.
Come now, my darlings… it shall not be long
Before we march again to battle songs.

ARMILUSTRIUM: an ancient Roman festival in honor of Mars, the god of war, on October 19
SCUTUM: large shield

You and Me

by Joe Tessitore

Some sins do not offend Our Lord—
in fact with mine, I think He's bored.
But sadly though, I must report
that yours are of a different sort.
They constitute the worst offense.
Your punishment will be intense
and last through all eternity—
how glad I am that I am me

and, truth be told, that you are you!
What more is there that I can do?
My every effort, you have spurned
and to me now, your back is turned.
Small wonder that you cannot see
the depth of my humility.

Surveillance, Twenty Twenty

by Joe Tessitore

I never thought I'd live to see
my TV looking back at me!

Two Limericks

by Joe Tessitore

My gender was never assigned,
so now I must make up my mind.
    I can do as God planned
    or take matters in hand
and risk going totally blind.

There once was a used-to-be man,
whose surgeon said "Yes dear, you can!"
    Though it's hard to believe
    he in fact did conceive
darling daughters named Harry and Stan!

The Limerick I'd Love to Write

by Joe Tessitore

There once was a President Trump
And many thought he was a chump.
    But none was more shrewd
    Than this big-city dude,
Now back over his wall they must jump!

Mosquitoes

by C.B. Anderson

I'd gladly give a pint or two a year—
extracted gently from my pulsing veins
by careful nurses tendering their dear
benignant ministrations—if it meant
I might then suffer less the little pains
and long anxieties for future bites
I'm subject to. They're not by accident,
but from a dipteran proclivity
for plaguing me on sultry summer nights
when sleeves are contraindicated. Why
those little devils must drill into me,
since I would freely share my body's sap
from china saucers, I don't know. I try
To sympathize, but more than not I slap.

First published in *Creosote*.

Epigrams on the Decay within Academia

by C.B. Anderson

Liberal Artifice

"Progressives," through advanced miseducation,
Have shaken our fair land to its foundation.

Gustatory Chiasmus

Good taste is timeless, sound, and with us always;
Good times are tasteless down collegiate hallways.

Lazy

The profs who plant their feet on vinyl hassocks
Are only fit for teaching ersatz classics.

Golden

What many teachers fail to recognize:
Cold silence is preferred to outright lies.

Superficial

The overarching underlying purpose
Of shallow thinkers is to scratch the surface.

The Ballad of Darryl O'Day

by Martin Hill Ortiz

There's a legend that's told in the neighborhood pubs,
In the smoke-filled gin joints and the posh country clubs,
In the places beer flows, be it froth or in dregs,
They say Darryl O'Day is the king of the kegs.

Now Darryl was sixty but still keeping fit;
His house by the brewer kept a hose joined to it.
With his kidneys still fearsome, his balance still fine:
When he chewed on a grape he could spit it out wine.

Yet, a decade had past since he'd fought for his title,
And a rumor went 'round that Darryl 'd grown idle.
Soon a brewhead named Stuart came after his throne.
From outside Darryl's window he made his claim known.

He cried to the world, "It's come time to acknowledge,
A new king's in town, I'm the champ of my college.
I maintain Darryl's finished, his panties are silk.
His head's full of glue and he drinks buttermilk!"
Darryl hadn't much words and had even less fear,
He said, "Let's settle this now, I've a brewery right here."

But Stu didn't answer: his visage fell flat.
He drank from the hose, then he turned and he spat.
First his face gave a twitch, then his neck made some twists,
His eyes became snakes and his hands became fists.

What was stewing in Stu only Stuart could say.
"This sissy-stuff brew, I could drink it all day.
If you want a real test," Stuart sneered in his anger,
"Then you'll come meet me down at the aeroplane hangar!"

What could Darryl do if not take up the bait?
With the town at his side he went after his fate.
He marched out to the hangar to meet with his peril:
A foul bubbling cauldron, a twelve-foot beer barrel.

'Twas an ale beyond pale, 'twas a beer so unfit,
It wore through the tongue that swore upon it.
A fermented, demented toxic-waste lager
Made part from old boots, and part gutter declogger.

Stuart paused to inhale, and then, licking his chops,
With a skip and a jump he went after those hops.
He chugged down eight quarts, and a pint and a gulp
'Til his legs turned to rubber, his brain to a pulp.
Soon swaying, displaying his snarl with a gat,
Still standing, demanding, said, "Darryl beat that."

Darryl sucked in his belly and tightened his bladder,
Then strolled to the wall where he set up a ladder.
With pretzel in teeth he climbed up to the rafters:
The crowd half in cheers and the other half laughter.

His mouth opened widely, the daredevil Darryl
Took a leap from his perch to plunge into the barrel.
He drank as he swam and he swam as he drank;
He made it look easy while draining that tank.
On down to a puddle he guzzled and slurped,
Then said, "What, no more?" out of grieving, he burped.

Then he sucked dry his clothes until no longer damp.
Just one drip remained: he who challenged the champ.
The crowd at first gasped, then hoorayed with a clangor,
And even Stu cheered from the floor of the hangar.

Throughout this wide world you'll find fools who are talky,
But there's damned few out there who can walk the Milwaukee.
So, wherever men teeter with wobbly legs,
They say Darryl O'Day is the king of the kegs.

Landscaping, or, How I Came to Believe in Global Warming

by Martin Hill Ortiz

I think that I shall never see
A tree that is invisible.
The very thought is risible—
Or maybe it's advisable
To say the word as "rīsible."

My crucial point is clear to see
—I mean it can be seen, not clear—
What's clear cannot be seen. I fear
I never saw but should have sawn
That tree that stood upon my lawn.

I blame my mirror with its missive:
Those objects far are near, or sort of.
And close? Remote!—or else just short of.
Which is to say I backed my car
Through objects near I thought were far.

And mirrors twist the world around!
When left is right then right's not rightful.
To spin the world is worse than spiteful:
This switch enables tricky trees
To hide in wait with seeming ease.

I barreled through a picket railing.
—In its defense, not much a fence—
I first de-fenced the fence and thence:
Invisible but sizeable,
A tree, unrecognizable.

Or else I'm blaming climate change.
So hot outside I took a drink,
No more than two, I'm sure, I think.
In seeing double, still unseen,
A tree lurked somewhere there between.

This global warming is a threat
Our fevered globe will be our doom:
The future's cloaked in lucid gloom.
What once was wood is now a clearing.
The trees, you see, are disappearing.

Slim Pickings

by David Whippman

His frame was gaunt, his income was erratic:
The crowd ignored the writer high above
Who wrote and brooded in his lonely attic,
Starving for beauty, poetry, and love.

These days, although his Muse is rather quiet,
The royalties and praises never cease.
He's found his niche, but needs to watch his diet—
The doctor says he's clinically obese.

Faith

by Mike Bryant

I'm pond scum, someone said today.
Some soup primordial, in a bay
was struck by lightning. Oh, I see
I'm wrought by electricity…
then, look! it's a bacterium
who, in a deep delirium,
decided he would rather be
a worm that crawls out of the sea.
From there it's just a natural flow
to Einstein, Michelangelo.

Or maybe, let's connect the dots,
we're spawned by ancient astronauts.
Of course, that doesn't answer where
they come from, maybe the thin air?
It's making perfect sense to me…
science answers perfectly.
If you don't think so, you're a dunce.
Regain your senses now, at once!
Just climb aboard and dance the dance,
and feel the will of circumstance.

(Science is the golden calf…
and God in Heaven has to laugh.)

Haiku

by W. "Cured Eel" Sabi (BDW)

I came to the sea.
I saw mountains of water.
I conquered nothing.

The fisherman drops
his line with bated breath down
to a certain depth.

Bits

by Paul Oratofsky

When memory's cleared I'd like to know
where all those bits of data go.
Do they have cozy homes with wives
where they live out their off-line lives?
And are they ready just in case
somewhere out in cyberspace
some dark, pernicious subroutine
needs bits of data in between
two saucy bytes in a nick of time
to set in place some algorhyme?
Will they be ready to obscene-
ly splash across some yokel's screen?
When memory's cleared dare I suppose
where all that information goes?

Don't Flog Yourself When Playing Golf

by Raymond Gallucci

A ball that's lost should never cost
    A one-stroke penalty.
Where now it dwells finds someone else—
    It's stolen property!

When perfect putt lips 'round the cup,
    No stroke need added be.
For physics claimed the putt was drained
    By law of gravity.

If hook or slice, it isn't nice
    To suffer grievously.
Don't blame your swing, 'cause frictioning
    Behaved mischievously.

Should drive you top or skyward pop,
    View not as casualty.
Seems underground some worm just found
    A way to move your tee.

Golf's sacred rules were made by fools
    Devoid of empathy.
So if you stink, don't even think
    That they apply to thee.

A Moving Experience

by Raymond Gallucci

We're the Stooges Three—your moving company.
If it ain't broke before we tote, it soon enough will be.

> Your furniture and prized possessions
> We handle as if our own.
> Employed, of course, movers' discretion
> When choosing which "Fragiles" are thrown.

We're the Stooges Three—your moving company.
We drop the ball on all we haul, then charge an extra fee.

> Your piano posed us not a problem.
> We do whatever we please.
> So why are you looking so solemn,
> So what if it's not in one piece?

We're the Stooges Three—your moving company.
You've tried the rest, can't pay the best, then we're your cup of tea.

> We trust that you'll give us a reference
> Whenever your friends need to move.
> We'll treat them with the same irreverence;
> We have a reputation to prove.

We're the Stooges Three—your moving company.
We haven't met a lawsuit yet from which we didn't flee.

Neil Armstrong (1930–2012)

by Martin Elster

You could fly while still growing and green,
could repair any flying machine
    by your twenties, and tested
    new rocket planes, crested
the clouds in your bright X-15.

In due course, you were picked for Apollo
(undreamed of by falcon or swallow)
    to land on the moon,
    and to do it quite soon
so the Commies could no more than follow.

You touched the moon's hide, took a stride,
spoke of steps and of leaps, then all pride
    disappeared as you turned
    towards your planet and learned
that your thumb is precisely as wide!

Albert Einstein (1879–1955)

by Martin Elster

A young-looking fellow employed
as a patent assessor enjoyed
    xperiments done
    in his head—lots of fun
for a purposeful, smart anthropoid.

He rode a light beam, thought of clocks
and a man in a plummeting box,
    but had very cold toes—
    which is just how it goes
when forgetting to bring your wool socks.

Views of gravity, light, time, and space
were suddenly new, and his face
    became famed as a lion
    and the stars of Orion
which, unlike his hair, know their place.

Poor Gluteus

by Connie Phillips

Alas, poor Gluteus!
    I had you at hello.
But everything has changed,
    As that was years ago.
I used to walk and run
    Or bike most everywhere,
But then I traded in
    My Nikes for a chair.
So comfy and so soft
    I didn't want to leave,
And never had the thought
    That I would be deceived.
And never did I think
    I'd be swept off my feet,
And so completely taken
    With a cushy seat!
And then, it was a car
    And benches, couches, stools…
Oh, I just didn't see
    I was a perfect fool!
But since I was so duped,
    Because I let you go,
I've nothing but regret
    And nothing now to show.
So people, listen up!
    It's not a piece of cake!
Ol' Gluteus needs help…
    Please learn from my mistake:
Don't let yourself get hooked
    On riding around town.
Dust off your sneakers now—
    Don't take it sitting down!

Et In Arcadia Ego

by Michael Coy

Oh, that's it, Keko. Pass through. Go ahead.
Just walk across my books without a glance,
with all that arrogant insouciance
of yours, encoded in that languid tread.

No, never mind that I've been up all night
engrossed in them. What now? So why the pause?
Ah, now I see. You might retract your claws
in expectation of a fondle-fight.

What must it be, to live a life by whim,
to eat, to sleep, to gambol, amble, bask
as humor takes you, never think to ask
of costs or consequences, to never trim

or balance, need to tack, or double back?
There's no one holding you to strict account.
You waste your time guilt-free, don't have to mount
defense or mitigation. If you lack

the cares and burdens of my tedious chores,
perhaps there's something else you'll never own—
a subtle thing called purpose, which alone
gives point to my percentages and scores.

Don't look so smug for landing on all fours!
This ledger's done. I know I have to die,
and that's my tragedy. You, pumpkin pie,
don't have a clue what's coming. And that's yours.

Mama

by Sally Cook

My mama took two drinks a year;
A shot glass down the gullet—
Yet hated bars and abhorred beer.
Would execute a pullet—
An ax, a stump—one frightened bird
Was done for in a minute,
Yet any gossip that she heard,
Would say there is no truth in it.

And on a dull November day,
You knew you'd find a cricket
Next to the fire, and she would say
There's good luck it brings with it.

Ladies did not lie or cheat—
If called for, though, they sometimes swore;
Did not partake of wild deer meat—
Those were the friends she had cared for.

She smoked a lot, and then she ground
The butts in a pale china hand—
Victorian symbol she had found—
The satire was not quite unplanned.

Was kind, and fed the transients,
Loved learning and the ancients.
For she was Mama, who I loved—
Who's burning stumps now, Up Above.

What We Have Come To

by Sally Cook

Now we will try to save the earth
By eating insects. What's it worth
To serve ourselves such awful chow?
We're cautioned that a gaseous cow
Can take away the oxygen.
Must give up oil, and coal, and then
Hope that the sun will shine each day,
Just hope; for Heaven's sake, don't pray
But watch the many windmills play
As ducks, unlucky, drop in thickets.
No matter, soon we'll snack on crickets
Roasted, dipped in chocolate sauce—
They're bugs, we're human—and we're boss!—

Self-Portrait 2005 by Steven J. Levin, 2005, oil on canvas, 40 x 32 in. Collection of the artist. (StevenJLevin.com)

HUMOR - JOURNAL VIII

Angus MacHartey's Final Party

a sequel to "Angus MacHartey's Final Party"

by Daniel Galef

Angus MacHartey's famous parties
Are terrors I've told you the tale of before.
The drinking and dancing go on for a week
And och aye! but the bastard lives next door.

I finally decided to attend
When Angus decided that what was needed
Was the Party to End All Parties—and
It may just have succeeded.

The guest list had no heavy-hitters,
No champions straight from the Highland Games,
No Rob Roy or Robert the Bruce:
Two first-rate men with four first names.

The Earl of Athole and some of his brose
Snapped at me like a tattie crisp.
All I said was "Hey there, Athole!"
How could he know about my lisp?

Lord Ullin's daughter seemed all washed up;
We called her the Caledonian Bore.
I finally met the real McCoy,
But I found I'd liked the phonies more.

And of all the devils that wander the moors,
Just who do you think decided to show?
The last person I wanted to see:
My ex—John Anderson my jo.

I got trapped in a droning sales pitch
From a timorous beast of a stuffed-kilt goon
Who kept trying to get me to invest in
The Banks o' Bonnie Doon.

The spread was McDonald's and Campbell soup,
As the caterers never showed up—how cheeky!
I asked the maid for some rumbledethumps,
But she left me with a cock-a-leekie.

It was doomed as soon as the whisky ran out:
It looked like enough to fill the lochs,
But, even though we poured it neat,
Soon the liquor supply was on the rocks.

MacHartey was doing whatever he could,
For his hype as a host was his only celebrity.
But plainly, poor old Angus was
More at-sea than an Outer Hebride.

After this bash, my neighbor dear
Has finally exhausted his revel reserves.
Old Angus has parted with parties for good,
And taken to bed with a case of nerves.

OCH AYE: oh yes
HIGHLAND GAMES: annual contest of Scottish games
ROB ROY: a Scottish folk hero, swashbuckling outlaw, and eponym of a very satisfying cocktail
ROBERT THE BRUCE: heavily mythologized Scottish king who fought with William Wallace
ATHOLE/ATHOLL: a historic earldom, now extinct
BROSE: a kind of porridge (Atholl brose is a traditional Scottish drink)
TATTIE CRISP: potato chip
LORD ULLIN'S DAUGHTER: a poem by Thomas Campbell ("'Come back, come back!' he cried in grief")
CALEDONIA: Scotland
CALYDONIAN BOAR: a monster in Greek mythology
REAL MCCOY: the genuine article

JOHN ANDERSON MY JO: a poem by Robert Burns ("But now your brow is beld, John")
TIMOROUS BEASTIE: from another poem by Robert Burns
THE BANKS O' DOON: another Burns poem
MACDONALDS AND CAMPBELLS: the most famous blood feud between Scottish clans, running for over 300 years after the Massacre of Glencoe
RUMBLEDETHUMPS: a dish of cabbage, onion, and mash
COCK-A-LEEKIE: "Scotland's National Soup," made from chicken and leeks
OUTER HEBRIDES: rocky islands off Scotland's northwest coast

Faust Money

by Daniel Galef

I sold my soul for silver.
In blood I signed my name.
I soon enjoyed the benefits of wealth, success, and fame.

I sold my soul for silver.
The day came to collect,
And I couldn't pay with cash or with renown or with respect.

I sold my soul for silver,
But, after it was sold,
I realized that I should have sold my soul for good old gold.

A Letter to Sir Grammar

by Dania El-Ghattis, high school poet

Dear Sir Grammar:
With all kindness and courtesy, may I request,
A new package of words, freshly made,
For, truly, it seems I have used them all up,
And my writing has near been betrayed.
To start with, I shall need a splatter of verbs,
That will glimmer and gleam for an age,
Then a handful of nouns, both concrete and abstract,
To bring pictures and life to my page.
Moving over and under, and round and about,
I shall need one or two prepositions,
And pronouns, though always unnamed and replacing,
They eliminate much repetition.
Next, a parcel of adjectives, crispy and sweet,
For those fellows sure love to explain.
Oh! And please don't forget to include interjections,
Those loud, lively words that exclaim!
Lastly, if you don't mind, I require some adverbs,
They're perfect for all types of weather,
And, always, please add in a ball of conjunctions,
To tie up my clauses together.
Now I must end this note, else my words all run out,
And if lucky, I'll manage to sign,
Dear Grammar, I thank you for these lovely phrases,
That make all the world's writing shine.

With the last of my words and I know it,
A very desperate poet.

Ode to a Car Key

by William Glyn-Jones

I.
O fine, faff-free, and labor-saving key
That lets me lock and unlock, with one press,
The car remotely and most easily
For you my heart now fills with thankfulness
    Let's say it's raining and one stands
        With luggage in both hands
It's been a busy day and one is tired
    How glad one feels to then recall
    A single button press is all
        That is required!

II.
Hephaestus for the gods with rarest skill
Did many a shining bronze device design
Some tool that leapt to action at their will
Performing tasks befitting lives divine:
    Their gold cars pulled by brazen steed
        Through air at such a speed
As lighting that precedes the thunder's rumble
    We feel ourselves to be their kin
    When gracefully we enter in
        Without a fumble.

III.
So unimpeded in the car I climb
And like a king upon a throne I sit
And cruise the country lanes in state sublime
Like Bacchus in his magic vine-filled ship
    And as my homeward way I wend
        I know at journey's end
There waits for me a happy circumstance:
    I'll loose the safety belt and out
    I'll get and walk away without
        A backwards glance.

Doomsday… or Not?

by Susan Jarvis Bryant

The Green New Deal is out there, and Bernie says it's true—
there's only twelve more years left for the likes of me and you
to curtail carbon footprints and cure the ailing earth
by living lives of paucity, deficiency, and dearth;
shunning all air travel to posh, exotic climes,
cooking on dung fires and shutting down the mines,
relishing bean burgers and banning buns with beef
coz cattle cutting cheese will bring apocalyptic grief;
trading roaring engines for sturdy walking shoes,
so long as they're not made from any bovine beast that moos.
Let's not forget the plastic and the drastic aftermath
of oil embroiled production that paved the green warpath;
so, switch off every cell phone and damn PCs to hell,
quit wittering on Twitter and break the Facebook spell;
turn off the heat and air-con, trade your brick house for a shack—
if you want a longer future you're compelled to travel back
to Neanderthal conditions, so now's the time to choose
to pine in pious penury, or crack a vat of booze,
then book a one-way ticket to an island soaked in sun
and bask in global warming for twelve more years to come!

Superfood Sonnet

by Susan Jarvis Bryant

When they deemed caffeine the health fanatic's fiend,
I dashed my skinny latte to the floor.
When my utter love of butter was demeaned,
I banned that spread from bread forevermore.
When chocolate was the rocky road to ills,
I blocked this shocking sin from drooling tongue.
On news that wine blinds minds and often kills,
I shunned my Chardonnay and Sauvignon.
But coffee's now the fitness guru's friend,
and butter is much better than once thought;
a chunk of chocolate they now commend,
And for prolonging life wine should be sought…

so, I'm scoffing and I'm quaffing as I chortle;
with my new menu, I'm sure to be immortal!

How Dare You, Santa! How Dare You!

by Susan Jarvis Bryant

Christmas has been canceled—it's naughty Santa's fault.
His haughty carbon footprint has been a grave assault
on melting polar ice caps; they're now a muddy puddle,
where sweaty elves and Rudolph are sizzling in a huddle.

Adios St. Nicholas, your super-speedy sleigh
should've been an eco-yacht; your flights have doomed the day!
The fun-fueled pixie factory packed with sacks of toys
is now a reindeer refuge—bah humbug, girls and boys!

Gone are high-tech headsets, transformers, trains, and drones,
Lego, Furbies, Barbies, Little Ponies, and iPhones,
all chock-a-block with plastic, all apt to shock the nose
of roving ocean turtles; such presents are their foes!

Snuff your Yuletide candle! Sling your Noel stocking!
Tear the tinsel from your tree! Stop the manger's rocking!
Toss the treetop fairy! Scrub the mistletoe!
Stuff your puffing chimney! There'll be no Ho Ho Ho!

Extinguish roasting chestnuts! Dump puddings plump with figs!
Quit crooning lilting carols! There'll be no choral gigs!
Free the fatted turkey! Cork the festive sherry!
Bolt your door! Flick off your lights! Box up all your merry!

So long to crass Kris Kringle, a climate refugee
washed up in a downtown bar in Memphis, Tennessee,
minus scarlet garb and beard, now sporting something spartan,
killing karaoke with strains of Dolly Parton!

Turkey Sausage

by Donald Carlson

The sausage on my plate is rubbery and inoffensive
A clever likeness made of turkey meat
Not your tastiest breakfast fare yet not complete-
Ly unsuitable for consumption by the hypertensive.
My research on this topic hasn't been extensive
But age and blood pressure require a retreat
From foods that I could once cavalierly eat
Without inflicting damage that might prove expensive.
Turkey sausage is the price of growing old—
As years increase so does the need to compromise
To dull our sharper joys with a dash of the bland.
Instead of calling life's bluff you tamely fold
Startled into timidity by the bracing surmise
That nothing's worked out quite the way you'd planned.

'Twas the Night Before Christmas

by Janice Canerdy

'Twas the night before Christmas and all through the malls
there was widespread confusion and hot, frenzied brawls.
Many shoppers were wanting the same bloomin' gifts.
Desperation resulted in feud-level rifts.
There were four grandmas fighting for one preschool game.
Their ferocity made angry pit bulls look tame.
Jostling shoppers collided and bags hit the floor.
Their attempts to retrieve them caused head butts and more.
Loud confusion—"That's mine!" "No, it's mine!!"—could be heard.
The mortified shoppers heard many a bad word.
Two old geezers that should have been home fast asleep
bumped into a Santa; all three muttered "BLEEP!"
When announcements "Ten minutes till close" hit their ears,
those who hadn't found all they desired held back tears.
The nightmare soon ended, tired shoppers went home,
Aware that at last no more malls they would roam.
Each vowed, "NO MORE last-minute shopping for me!"
Christmas morning—well-rested—all smiles by the tree,
they remembered the monsters they'd been just last night
and rejoiced that those creatures were nowhere in sight!

The Melancholy Snowman

by Theresa Zappe

Though stony-eyed, I watched the finches glide.
The chimney smoke, the builder slide,
At night, I gave the constellations words,
The House, the Builder, and the Birds.
My silver ear was filled with tree-ish taps,
And twiggy fingers twitched with sap,
I wondered if the rain would melt my heart,
When, at a loss, I dripped apart.
And then I found the key to my creation,
There at the edge of transformation,
I lost my head, but heard a peeper sing,
And that made sense of everything!

Withering Slights

by Michael Glassman

I start to age ten minutes out of bed,
More fragile now but not yet dead.
My son-in-law hovers 'round me when I walk
In case I stumble as we talk.
My daughter's gift to me: a three-pronged cane
Concealed within the quiche Lorraine.
A stranger volunteers his seat to me.
The spine's the bane of the elderly;
L4 and L5 express their relief
At respite for their commander-in-chief.
Since others hold a door with a "There you go,"
Call me "Papa" as I walk slow,
And tell me that "The door button's on the left,"
I go home feeling less bereft.

Homophonic Poetry

O Deer, thou lissome spirit of the wood
I see thee now a-leaping in a free way!
Oh dear. If I were you I never would
Have leaped into the middle of the freeway.

—William Glyn-Jones

A fly told a flea what to do:
"If you fly, keep that vent in your view."
But the poor flea was ailing,
the tip unavailing.
It flew with the flu in the flue.

—Mark F. Stone

"Sheesh," she shed a tear upon the tier,
Which stood above the pier on which the Peer
(He was a prince) left finger prints (Oh, dear)
Upon the antlered carcass of a deer
That had been gently laid upon a bier.
"Let's drink a toast," he said, and raised a beer.
"To everybody here I say, 'Hear! Hear!'"

—James A. Tweedie

A frosty Highlands sky
Caught Scots by surprise.
When asked, one man said, "Aye,
I see icy eyes."

—James A. Tweedie

I saw a bare bear
and a hare without hair
on the stair—did I stare?
Oh yeah!

I spied with shy eye,
sidled by to go buy
underwear for the daring pair.

"Was it dear, deer?" they said
with cheeks blushing red
at the price tag they read—
Oh yeah!

But, I'm a doe in the know
with a dough-splashing beau
who never says no coz he's fair.

A toad towed them home
in a cart with a groan
from a hoarse horse who waived the fare.
"Cheap! Cheap!" the birds cheeped.

"Bald! Bald!" bawled the beasts.
"Please! Please!" rose my pleas, "Spare a care
for the bare bear and hare without hair!"
Oh yeah!

—Susan Jarvis Bryant

"A Line of Shakespeare" Contest Winners

"2B or not 2B, that is the question"
The driver faced upon his wife's suggestion
That in the mall's garage, he'd lost his way,
and needed to ascend to level "A."

—Martin Rizley, from *Hamlet*

"Shall rotten death make conquest of the stronger?"
Never! While Faith still lives and hearts are pure,
The flame of Western triumph shall endure
And courage strengthen where the odds are longer.

—Franklin P. Scudder, from *The Rape of Lucrece*

"Love alters not with his brief hour and weeks,"
And works for introverts, as well as geeks,
Who may not say a lot… but when they do!
Each word of passion resonates as true.

—David Watt, from "Sonnet 116"

"The lady doth protest too much, me thinks."
She still contests the vote and says it stinks
that Trump won in an underhanded way.
But who paid for the FISA dossier?

—Mark F. Stone, from *Hamlet*

IV. EXPOSING COMMUNISM

Hong Kong protest image
(StandWithHK.org/us)

Leveled Outcomes

by Charlie Bauer

Philosophers of Marxist ilk designed
For leveled outcomes, then they slew en masse.
It pleased the Nazi socialists to grind
Up twenty million lives—hence, Zyklon gas.

The Russian cognoscenti chose to build
A communistic state; death charmed again.
The truth (not Pravda) is that Stalin killed
Nine million lives: young children, women, men.

In China, Mao took hold and planned his Great
Leap Forward; peasant hope became despair
As forty million workers met their fate.
Dead students' shades still haunt the Beijing Square.

In Stalin's words: "One death is tragedy,
One million's a statistic"—none would see.

She Walked in Beauty

a tribute to Gao Rongrong* after Lord Byron's "She Walks in Beauty"

by Connie Phillips

She walked in Beauty, pure as light—
Like sun and moon and starlit skies
Illuminate the darkest night…
Such was the brightness of her eyes
And shining smile of sheer delight
That all would pause when she passed by.

With faith in Truth, Compassion, and
Forbearance firm within her heart,
Steadfast like diamond is to sand,
She rose above to stand apart;
Though suffering at Evil's hand,
Her innocence would ne'er depart.

Assailed by Evil's vicious blows,
To its demands she'd not submit.
Instead, 'midst pain, she bravely chose
To use her life—each breath of it—
And to the world the crimes expose
Of communism's biggest twit.

True Beauty's light shall never fade,
While Evil in the ground is laid.

---

*Gao Rongrong was a Falun Gong practitioner who was tortured to death by the Chinese communist regime because of her beliefs. She had her family secretly take photos of her mutilated face and use them to expose the persecution of Falun Gong, which was launched on July 20, 1999, and still continues to this day.

For Falun Gong

by David Whippman

Their plight is real, their cause is ours.
So far, alas, the "great and good"
Show no concern, although they should:
No virtue-signaling movie stars.

Although the world's eyes look elsewhere,
The cause of Falun Gong is just.
In we, their friends, they have to trust:
For them, our friends, we have to care.

How long must they endure? How long?
The will for change is what we need,
Let's play our part by word and deed
And help the folk of Falun Gong.

Winner of the Friends of Falun Gong 2019 Poetry Competition (fofg.org)

Mother of Falun Gong

by Gleb Zavlanov

They said my mother would be back tomorrow,
They said her smile would still shine proudly here,
Her hand brush off the dreadful, bitter sorrow
That manifests itself within a tear,
But twenty years had faded like wan mists
That glide and winnow on a brackish lake,
And yet, her awful absence still persists
And strives and strains to make my small heart break.

Where is she? *She is gone, dear, precious heart,*
And gone as well the heart she used to own,
The heart that throbbed, the heart that took a part
In you and warmed you when you felt alone,
The heart, your mother's once, found beating now
Within a stranger's breast, but where is she?
Where is your mother? Where that empty vow
Of her return? It all rings hopelessly.

No more those dreams, wake up! No more those visions.
Dead lies your mother, flickered out her life,
One pure belief, a thousand deep incisions,
The workings of a government's cold knife.
They killed her, knocked her dead, wormed through her skin;
They let her seething blood spill like your tear,
Killed in a world in which no one may win
But suffer for the values they hold dear.

EXPOSING COMMUNISM - JOURNAL VIII

Freed by Faith by Xiaoping Chen, 2006, oil on canvas, 30 x 62 in. A Falun Gong practitioner walks out of a Chinese labor camp. Based on a true story.

Forgetting the Tiananmen Square Massacre for 30 Years

by Damian Robin

Robbed of life and liberty in open air,
Young citizens ran out of breath inside the Square.
Hot bullets opened skin to pump bright flesh holes bare.
A follow-up of tanks made sure no space was spare.
The man who shuffled shopping bags and stopped a tank
Stayed famous 30 years although his presence sank
As slickly as the fleshy dead who never stank
But were removed, like hidden debt in some big bank.
The daylight robbery that's laundered by the state
Removing people's histories and aired debate
Has no remorse or memories to show to date
In law courts, government departments, embassies,
Confucius Institutes, and universities.
That forced amnesia: the communist disease.

Towards the End of Chinese Communism

by Damian Robin

Through Shanghai's packed glissando peaks and Beijing's glossy miles,
As though to keep out counter breaths and polish glassy smiles,
The dazing days of blinding fogs form fumes like whiskey casks,
And crowds wear masks like masks still worn for organ harvest tasks.
Stretched fencing cranes brick up grave holes in deep construction sites

Dank cuts of meat and fly-tip slops no human ever bites
Steam cook in dumpsters clogging backs of restaurants and shops…
Here anyone who says what's what is taken for the chop.
As Chinese 'round the world are tracked, the living and the dead,
The CCP's cold genocides that poison what gods fed
Are swallowed in Divinity as Wholesome Light extends
And manifests in Falun Gong and all of Heaven's friends.

CCP: Chinese Communist Party

Party Terrorists

by Damian Robin

Disguised and tooled-up army terrorists
Floor trapped citizens and lash their wrists.

Police in protest clothes mash down the young:
Trojan houseflies on a honeyed tongue.

Wild triad sticks swish tee-shirts wet with cries,
Innocents in subways caught by spies.

At pressure points sit Hong Kong socialists
Ticking wishes on the Party list.

On Viewing the Image of a Dead Hong Kong Protester

by Joseph S. Salemi

I blame the Brits. In '97
Hong Kong was a bit of heaven.
Prosperity and freedom reigned—
Speech was never kept restrained.
The people were at peace. What's more,
They hoped that, just like Singapore,
They might become a full-fledged state
To save them from the horrid fate
Of being grabbed by Commie claws
And living under leftist laws.
But our British friends finked out.
They didn't have the guts or clout
To tell the Commies to piss off.
All they did was hem and cough
And dither in vague indecisions.
They should have sent a few divisions
Of crack troops, plus a naval fleet
And told Beijing "We won't retreat—
We owe it to the people here
Who cherish freedom. Is that clear?"
Instead, the British lion mewed.
And folks in Hong Kong now are screwed.

(My apologies to James Sale. Nothing personal is meant.)

Why Not?

by T.M. Moore

We shake our heads, and wonder, "Why?" aloud
each time some speeding truck plows through a crowd,
or grinning gunman gloats at blood and breath
spilled and extinguished by his date with death;
or when some faithless man, supposing life
is little more than sex, discards his wife
and children, showing not the least remorse;
and when some jackboot beats a saint—or worse—
we look the other way, or maybe pray
and shrug, not knowing what to do or say.
For we have tolerated, without much
objection, all the many lies that clutch
our throats with ever-tightening grip, as by
our shameful, silent sufferance we comply
with those who teach that life is meaningless,
and satisfying self's the way to bless
your nonexistent soul; who bloviate
on moral duty while they tolerate
whatever new morality some fool
in academic garb touts as a rule
of life; and who, like us and all the rest,
care only for whatever suits them best.
So when mind-boggling sadnesses occur,
and minds grope vainly, and the truth's a blur,
instead of asking "Why?" we really ought,
all things considered, ask ourselves, "Why not?"

The Cell Tells

by Angel L. Villanueva

Unwise are those who spread unfettered lies,
Who claim that life arose from lifeless ooze.
They choose to see with Darwin's blinded eyes,
So fail to note creation's many clues.

They mock the thought that life had guiding hands,
That God designed and breathed life into man.
To boundless chance they bow as ardent fans,
Rejecting truth that tells how life began.

The humble human cell cries out to them
To seek and search within its guarded halls,
For there is found design that will condemn
The lies retold and writ on wobbly walls.

His wondrous work they view with blindfold eyes,
While sipping barren brew from Darwin's lies.

"Made in China"

by Randal A. Burd, Jr.

"Made in China" reads the label—
Shattered on the coffee table:
Some cheap and broken plastic toys
We purchased for our girls and boys—
Imports purchased which enable

Labor camps that leave unstable
Lives in ruin and can disable
Limbs... but disregard the noise
Made in China.

Are our children really stable?
We disservice and mislabel
All the little girls and boys
Who grow up with cheap plastic toys;
Sold our souls and bought a fable
Made in China?

To Know the Mobs of Modern Days

dedicated to my wife, who was mobbed and defamed for political gains

by Jared Pearman

They've come before with pitchforks high,
With torches beaming off their knives.
This time they come instead with phones
To kill my queen and steal her throne.

No lynch mobs now or guillotine,
Just accusations on a screen.
They change the meaning of our words,
Then backdate crimes, it's so absurd.

Last time they called us bourgeoisie.
This time it could be anything.
"A rightist, witch, supremacist!"
Once they name you, you're on a list

Of those who don't deserve defense,
And no one cares if it makes sense.
Their hate comes first and truth comes last—
No concern for the new outcasts.

But names and words are all they know,
Devoid of meaning, all for show.
Ten good people they will destroy,
Their claims of virtue, just a ploy.

To cover up their true intent—
To ruin the world they resent.
"Yes, I'm the victim," they proclaim,
While sucking blood from those they've named.

EXPOSING COMMUNISM - JOURNAL VIII

It matters not what song they sing
In Salem, Paris, or Beijing.
They only want to feed their hate,
To watch you burn upon their stake.

Sadistic wolves as lambs disguised,
Behind great words their malice hides.
So now we watch the mobs return,
Because it seems we never learn.

Capitulation never works.
It only ever makes things worse.
Each time that we apologize
For some imaginary crime,

Or fail our friends in moments meek,
We give these mobs the blood they seek,
And like young Kirsten Dunst they say,
"I want some more," and more each day.

Saint Joan of Arc they burned alive—
So many Christians crucified.
Socrates they poisoned too.
See the pattern? I hope you do.

"A heretic!" the crowds will shout
At anyone who dares to doubt,
Or who has courage in spite of pain
To speak true words while Truth remains.

Should all beauty and words most wise
Be torn from books and branded lies?
Should all our reason be denied
In acquiescence to their chides?

These mobs just want more points to score
In pointless, aimless online wars.
Do not give in to empty threats.
You'll die with nothing but regrets.

Beware attempts to rewrite our past—
To have traditions be recast.
We've learned so much through history—
So much of it in misery.

Forgotten are the lessons learned
Through many wars and prophets burned.
Divinity is all that saves
Humanity from being slaves.

Stop Communism in the Philippines poster, U.S. government, 1951.

The Cost of Free Money

by Philip Keefe

When man is given everything he needs
The motivation for his labor ends;
Sufficiency to idle living leads,
As want upon deficiency depends.
While soporific thoughts pervade his mind
Remaining diligence will be the cost,
And when he's by his indolence defined,
From others and himself, respect is lost.
Less favored man must work an honest day
Before he can enjoy some hours of rest;
Yet his reward's much greater than his pay,
Of dignity and pride he is possessed.
    Perhaps it's there a golden lesson lies:
    It's not a life of ease that satisfies.

V. PRO-LIFE

Massacre of the Innocents by Angelo Visconti, 1860–1861,
oil on canvas, 3.95 x 2.93 in.

In the Garden

by Joe Tessitore

In Paradise there is a place
where ruby-colored roses grace
the trellises of precious pearl—
so splendidly their buds unfurl!

She and her Child oft' wander here
among the flowers they hold dear
and with their sacred presence bless
each fragrant bloom with tenderness.

Ever now in heavenly light
because they were denied the right
by we who would their lives destroy
to be a little girl or boy.

No matter how we misconstrue;
indeed, we know just what we do.

Haiku

by Joe Tessitore

When a newborn cries,
locked in a room by itself,
does it make a sound?

The Black Children

by J. David Graham

In China, until rather recently,
each pair of parents was allowed one kid,
according to the "one-child policy."
Some parents had another, which they hid.
Unregistered, these kids are sometimes sold
to traffickers who make them prostitutes.
If they refuse, they're left out in the cold;
thus little girls are raped by savage brutes.
The Communists refuse them legal aid;
they call these children "black," deny their life,
deny them rights, deny them getting paid,
deny them education, give them strife.
Despite all this, these children still exist;
To save them from this hell, we must persist.

Cleve Backster

by Evan Mantyk

While people claim the fetus has no being
Worth enough to trump a mother's rights,
There's something more our human eyes aren't seeing:
Life's more, not less, when we adjust our sights.

The year abortion gained the courts' accord,
He told the world that plants have in their souls
Emotions—lie detectors can record—
Perceptions, feelings, interactive roles.

But ambled in the scoffing scientists
Who said, "Great claims require great evidence,"
And failed to see that unseen life resists
Control that gives us humans confidence.

The greatest confidence should be in life;
It's not something to doubt, but that is rife.

Cleve Backster's work on plant perception gained wide exposure in the 1973 publication *The Secret Life of Plants*.

Personhood

—noun 1. "the state or fact of being a person."

by Ron L. Hodges

"Person," it seems, is an elusive word,
Though I am rather puzzled as to why.
Isn't membership in the human herd
Sufficient cause to make that term apply?
Apparently not. Many will dispute,
Saying a "person" must do that or this,
Look a certain way; life alone is moot
If any standard markers are amiss.
But since these self-styled experts don't agree
On what constitute those minimum traits,
Should we define with ambiguity?
I fear we're playing gods with people's fates—
Personhood can't be some subjective prize,
Earned through the fickle measures men devise.

The Life That Is Not Life

"I'm getting ready for my trip now." —Aurelia Brouwers
(who chose to be euthanized at age 29 in the Netherlands)

by Ron L. Hodges

You said it was the humane thing to do
    For those condemned to "endless pain and strife,"
Yet did you ever pause to ponder who
    Would be assigned "the life that is not life"?

You said it would end hardship without hope,
    Spare those doomed the indignity of fate;
You scorned any fear of an unseen slope
    As mere lunacy, nothing to debate.

So, when asked where the margin would be drawn
    Across this dim continuum of death,
You refused to render a Rubicon;
    Instead, you gave some airy shibboleth.

"When a life is no longer life," you said,
    "That's the standard society will use,"
Careless that lurking in the haze ahead
    There might be a shadow we could abuse.

Yes, here where the dignified dead began,
    The epitaphs lend credence to your claim—
Futures hopeless, and more suffering than
    Any mortal medicine could tame.

Yet, in the Cemetery of Mercy,
    A darkness looms down there—below the rise.
That's where the markers of this grassy sea
    Betray what pain-avoidance will devise.

PRO-LIFE - JOURNAL VIII

The gravestones multiply like cancer cells,
    But not for cureless cancers do they bloom;
More and more the terminal tale each tells
    Is enduring sadness, not certain doom.

Let me show you an alcoholic one
    Who simply chose to forego the fight,
Or another for whom the brightest sun
    Could never seem to penetrate with light.

Others unalterably defective,
    (At least they perceived their own flaws that way),
And elder souls possessing years to live
    Convinced not to burden another day.

Oh, and look! Sprouting there—a newborn grave!
    Let's examine this late resident's grounds.
Let's see what made the inhabitant crave
    A permanent home in an earthen mound.

A pink-and-red stuffed dinosaur stands guard
    Beside the gravestone of its fallen friend;
How can a visitor's nerves not be jarred
    By what this childish token might portend?

And, behold, the writing upon the stone,
    The epitaph so delicate and fine—
Oh, Aurelia, your fate was unknown,
    And you were still young—merely twenty-nine!

Is it compassion to let someone die
    When suffering springs from a troubled mind?
Is it unmerited to question why
    We mock slippery slopes while roaming blind?

You said it was the humane thing to do
    For those condemned to "endless pain and strife,"
Yet did you ever pause to ponder who
    Would then assume "the life that is not life"?

Room 402: Gehenna Comes to New York

On Governor Andrew Cuomo's Jan. 22, 2019 repeal of New York's Public Health Law § 4164

by Amy Foreman

The children of her forebears died
    more expeditiously
when fires of infanticide
    consumed them viciously.

Oh, sure, they suffered in the haze
    of smoke and drums and song,
but life surrendered to the blaze
    of heat before too long.

Each spirit quit its tiny frame
    of flesh, so charred and black.
The mercy of the eager flame
    lies in its swift attack.

It's cold in Molech's hands today;
    she startles, shivers, stills
upon the counter in a tray
    of blood that quickly chills.

Once swaddled warmly in the womb,
    now naked, head to toe,
extracted to this sterile room
    about an hour ago.
"No doctors will be called," they said,
    while cleaning up the mess.
"In just a moment she'll be dead;
    we'll call this a success."

And now they've left; the door is shut;
    the lights have been turned off:
Room 402 abandoned, but
    she waits, in stainless trough

for Tophet's god to stop the breath
    within her lungs so small.
This isolated, frigid death
    is cruelest of them all.

POET'S NOTES: "Room 402" does not refer to any specific event happening in a certain room, but was chosen at random to represent any room in which a late-term abortion takes place. "Gehenna" and "Tophet" are biblical metonyms for hell, and also refer to a valley near Jerusalem where Israelites once participated in the sacrifice of their own children, burning them alive in the hands of the Canaanite idol Molech (also Moloch, Malcam, or Milcom).

These Twins

by Leo Zoutewelle

These twins came forth in one amniotic sac.
They sensed the danger they had come upon
And both held hands to keep that danger back:
It truly was the best they could have done.
Their need for holding hands kept them in place
Until the water broke at last at birth,
And all gave heartfelt thanks to this, God's grace,
Which gave them blissful love and loving mirth.
They now hold hands with joy most all the time,
And know each other's thoughts without a sound;
They know they hurt when separate, and pine,
Yet, ever close, by total love are bound.
But why do I now think of Margaret Sanger?
Whose name forever rhymes with "coat hanger."

Abortion Rights—Murder

lyrics inspired by the movie Unplanned

by Edward C. "Ted" Hayes

Ms. Sally loved the parties, spent her nights out "on the town."
Her door was open for the boys, whenever they came 'round.
Then one morning when she woke, she knew that things weren't right;
She punched up numbers on her phone, and called "Abortion Rights."
They sympathized and named a friendly obstetrician man.
He met her with a smile, and hypodermic in his hand.
She felt a shock, the womb convulse, and then a searing pain.
The child was born, and gave a cry—and never cried again.

>It's called "abortion rights"
>No one would ever dare…
>To call it—murder

Every doctor takes an oath to do the very best he can
To do no harm, and most stay true, in this once Godly land,
But some inject a mother so the child within her womb
Is born, a lifeless corpse, and stacked like garbage in the room.

>It's called abortion rights,
>And none would ever dare…
>To call it—murder

There are some that some call "doctor," and some gov'nors in our land
Who hide the truth in silken words, so we won't understand.
They say, "Comfort the newborn"—what a mockery of words!
They mean, "A pillow on its face, the choking won't be heard."

>They call that "comforting"
>They say "abortion rights"
>They know it's—murder

VI. OBSERVATIONS

A Poet by Jean-Louis Ernest Meissonier, 1859,
oil on canvas, 22 x 16 in.

The Fate of Fine Art

by Peter Hartley

Too late to turn the clock back on fine art,
Egregious oxymoron that it may
Be called today, but where to find the start
Of this, the slow beginnings of decay?

For once we found our world inside the space
That we saw bounded by a frame. The height
Of charm resided in the commonplace
Where now the commonplace is merely trite.

And in that world we knew the things we felt,
We recognized, the life we saw and thought
We knew, the things we touched and heard and smelled
And learned and read, the things that we'd been taught.

And then it seems the Fauvist movement came
Along, divorcing outline, color, shade,
And form, each from the other. Should we blame
Matisse, for one, the hotchpotch he portrayed?

Technique and skill no longer score in art,
Nor presentation. Concept counts for all.
When craft in execution lost its part,
For art it proved the writing on the wall.

Today's great works of art are meant to shock,
Are often vulgar, utterly debased,
Designed to ape the loathsome, out to mock
The twee and every benchmark of good taste.

The more ephemeral a work of art,
Like children's castle carvings in wet sand,
The greater chance that it will fall apart,
The higher price it seems it will command.

Artists today will brush aside our fears
Of transience. They've no concern, at heart,
For what effect will have the passing of the years
On shoddy work and shoddy works of art.

Long gone the days when artists would have ground
And bound their own pigments, who had the sense
To choose the methods that they found were sound
While having due regard to permanence.

No more can art astound us or confound
Our visual acuity or raise
Perceptions and our awe, where once we found
That it would open up our eyes, amaze

Us, make us look and look again in ways
We couldn't see till artists lent their sight
To us and then on nature we would gaze
Anew to see more clearly in the light.

As poetry today must be opaque,
Have scant regard for scansion, feet, or rhyme,
So too in art the rules that we can break
Can only lead to anarchy in time.

A bandwagon for those without restraint,
A permit to create without constraint,
A license to bespatter, daub, and taint
Their canvases with cheap emulsion paint.

Too late to rescue art from all the wrong
Publicity it draws, the ridicule,
Perplexity, and disbelief along
With scorn for what shows not a minuscule

Amount of talent or ability.
The cutting edge of art today is all

About sensation and celebrity
And arrogance, audacity, and gall.
It shows how far the talentless can stretch
The boundaries of what they're able to:
Some wretch can spend five minutes on a sketch
That ends up as a seminal breakthrough

For vorticist post-futuristic art.
An etching smaller than a postage stamp
In fetching multi-squillions, apart
From all the kudos for the little scamp,

It gets his latest retrospective flown
To all the seven continents and sent
Off to the Venice Biennale, shown
At every single pseudo-art event.

Why paint a portrait of a man and try
To catch his likeness if you can? Just do
A daub with jumbo dung and let it dry,
Entitle it "Untitled, Number Two."

If only artists could just stand apart
From flagrant self-advertisement and hype
And put more effort into so-called art
They'd churn out ten times more appalling tripe.

TWEE: quaint, pretty, or sentimental

The Plight of Animals

by Peter Hartley

The plight of animals, how must it be
Ordained thus, either by a just God or
A merciful? By nature meek and poor,
They have no hopes, no future can they see
And all they own their living now as we.
No retrospect, their past is nevermore,
Their present short, a wretched end in store
Though dear their lives to them as mine to me.

Our ends will come, in torment or at peace,
For we too hold mere tenure of a lease,
Yet proudly we alone anticipate
A future life if we can expiate
The past. But why are helpless beasts outcast,
And who will give the sinless peace at last?

Love of Life

by David Paul Behrens

How I long for the days gone by,
Such memories overtake me.
I look back on my life and sigh,
May the future not forsake me.

All the fond thoughts of yesteryear,
Coupled with the thoughts of regret;
Love of life is ever so near,
It captures my soul like a net.

So many things I could have done,
But I did not follow through.
Maybe I walked, but should have run;
Such thoughts hang pale and blue.

The sun still shines, up in the sky,
The moon is still glowing at night.
Life goes on, regardless of why,
And the darkness turns into light.

All in all, life is still worthwhile,
Happiness remains in my sight.
Some things I recall, make me smile;
My love of this life shines bright.

'Tis Better

by Joe Tessitore

What is there that is not divine?
And so this life, it is not mine
but gift indeed, meant to be shared
and from this calling, none are spared.

So answer with no thought of cost;
to hesitate is to be lost.
Open your hearts and they will fill
with treasures that enchant and thrill.

Neither to hoard nor ours to keep;
the good is here for all to reap.
What you bestow, He will restore
with best of measure, running o'er.

Live by His words; in them believe:
"Better to give than to receive."

Rimini

by Joseph Charles MacKenzie

I stand before the Adriatic Sea,
Unwreathed of confidence in things to be,
Time's wind-born song of spray and transient foam
With each wave's death dies one more death in me.

Behind, the glories of eternal Rome;
Above, a blank morn's achromatic dome;
Below, the ebb and flow of all my days,
A distant sail, a vagrant thought of home.

I stand, a rock beneath the bone-blanched haze;
Lost eons rustle sand beneath my gaze;
The salt-breeze asks where all my Aprils fled,
And where my hopes, and where my fleeting Mays.

I ponder paths abandoned, where they led,
The swell of life, the outflow of the dead
Who wait to waken where their gray stones lie,
And muse on what might stir a dreamless head.

The green sea groans a long and wistful sigh;
The chant of fishermen draws near, and I
Wait on for thee, the sun my sea would wed,
One day, beneath a resurrected sky.

The Fall of the Fourth Estate

by Randal A. Burd, Jr.

The Media: the Fourth Estate*
Performed disgracefully of late:
Delivering the news askew,
Allowing certain viewpoints through
To fuel the discontent and hate.

Campaigning bullies will berate
The citizens and educate
Their friends to start deferring to
The Media.

All politicians propagate
Hypocrisy and subjugate
Constituents with their worldview
While building up their revenue,
And few are eager to negate
The Media.

---

*"The Fourth Estate" is a term attributed to British politician Edmund Burke in 1787, referring to the press as a political force whose influence is not consistently or officially recognized.

Humilitas

by Randal A. Burd, Jr.

There is this hope they will remember me,
While not with flags half-lowered on the pole,
As someone they would all aspire to be:
A model man—another kindred soul.

Intentions were befouled by circumstance.
Accomplishments seem slight when said aloud.
But when I failed to seize a second chance,
I still survived unbroken and unbowed.

There will be those who mark my death with tears
As substance passes quickly into shade;
I pray they judge my time productive years
And face their circumstances unafraid.

I leave this life to stand before a gate
And pray to God my name's upon the scroll,
That afterlife may grant a better fate
Than I deserve in judgments of the soul.

The Captain to His Mate

by Randal A. Burd, Jr.

These days I often pause to contemplate
How fortunate I am to share with you
Our struggles overcome which left our fate
Unbroken by the tempests rolling through.
God knows some days we've been denied a breeze;
However, we've survived the strongest gales
To right the ship and head for calmer seas,
Fair winds be damned as we unfurled the sails.
Until our voyage runs its natural course,
Land-sightings will be few and far between.
No hurricane or like destructive force
Exists to make our journey less serene.
So long as you are with me on this trip,
Survival means I won't give up the ship.

Venting

Be angry, and do not sin. —Ephesians 4:26

by T.M. Moore

We're told a large volcano roils and seethes
beneath the soil of Yellowstone. The steam
that rises all throughout the park, and wreathes

its many pools and vales, would surely seem
to validate that claim. Word is, that should
that angry monster find an open seam

and rush the surface all at once, it would
erupt with so much force and power that, well,
let's say not much would come of it of good.

The beast is vented, else it would be hell
to pay. Its geysers and its bubbling pools
release the pressure, so it doesn't swell

to bursting, which it would without these tools.
And what of all the rage that festers in
my soul? One trusty mechanism rules

that ugly beast and keeps it chained within
the dark recesses of my heart. I know
my anger would erupt, give way to sin,

but for this outlet, this release valve. So
I write, and writing lets me let it go.

Dust

My soul clings to the dust. —Psalm 119:25

by T.M. Moore

How like the dust my soul can be. I see
it sometimes, dazed and inattentive in
a ray of light, or settled in a thin
coat on a table, waiting languidly
to be wiped off. It falls in easily
with just the slightest breeze or passing wind,
and drifts off nowhere, much to my chagrin.
Such aimless, listless seasons trouble me.

Perhaps it's true that I am merely dust.
But even dust has purpose, and I trust
that, in my more devoted moments, when
I'm neither drifting, dazed, nor lolling, then
I'll shimmer in the light, and lend my weight,
though slight, to tip the scales for something great.

OBSERVATIONS - JOURNAL VIII

Notre-Dame by Lin Petershagen, 2019, acrylic painting on canvas, 19.7 x 27.6 in. (LinPetershagen.com)

The Cathedral, Burning

by T.M. Moore

Flames wreck the walls and ceilings that had stood
for centuries, scorch ancient timbers, raze
to ash that sanctuary made for praise,
and cruelly crumble sacred stone and wood
that neither wars nor revolutions could
bring down. And there—where holy hands would raise
in faith, and trusting saints sang lays
while incense spread a holy fragrance, good
and pure—dark, dreary smoke swells like a flood,
obscuring light and glory in thick haze
and ugly, bullying billows. No one prays,
but everybody weeps, as well we should,
    to see the flames of lust and lies that scathe
    the trust of innocents, and wreck their faith.

Reparations

Owe no one anything but to love one another. —*Romans 13:8*

by T.M. Moore

What shallowness, what an impoverished view
of human life, that reckons men to be
machines that will dispense whatever we
desire if only we are careful to
insert the right amount of cash. That peace
and justice can be purchased like a soft
drink or a bag of chips should well be scoffed
at. Do we really think the rage will cease
once reparations checks have been received?
Do we so little understand the soul
that we think this new version of the dole
will satisfy those who have been aggrieved?
   The currency we need to satisfy
   this debt is sadly in too short supply.

Luckily for the Lovelorn

by E.V. Wyler

Luckily for the bereft
grieving through darkness alone,
dawn is abundantly deft
at its medicinal tone.

When a new morning appears,
duty abruptly commands
focusing thoughts on careers
and some routinized demands.

During distressing ordeals,
structural chores are, of course,
spokes on restorative wheels,
turning with rhythmical force...

Familiar labors assigned
(whether unique or mundane)
comfort the crestfallen mind
like an elixir for pain.

Physical efforts promote
pleasing endorphins to rise.
Mental endeavors demote
misery's spirit and size.

Affable people abound,
sharing benevolent goals.
Meaningful purpose is found,
forged in incredible roles.

Muscular hearts can attest
circular time is renowned
for its centrifugal zest,
helping the lovelorn rebound!

Let Me Go Gentle into That Dark Night

after Dylan Thomas

by Rohini Sunderam

Let me go gentle into that dark night,
Let me not rage against the dying light;
There is another light that beckons me
That from this garish light will set me free.
It softly glows and grows on that far side;
I hear a hymn that sings with me abide.
Let me go gentle into that dark night.

I will not rage against the close of day;
Let me be like a glowing sunset, pray,
Sending colors of every rainbow hue
From brightest red up to the deepest blue;
Let me learn from the deathbed of the sun
To leave the light and from its brightness run.
Let me go gentle at the close of day.

Now, loved ones, let me wish you fond farewell
The time is right; I hear the tolling bell;
It's not a knell, it has a happy ring
Like Christmas bells and voices caroling.
My heart towards that call is rushing now
I've lived my life; please let me take that bow
And let me gently wish you all farewell.

The Loan

a villanelle

by Benjamin Daniel Lukey

This life we hold so dear is but a loan.
For good or ill, its balance must be spent,
For life is not a thing that we can own.

The wasting of our fragile flesh and bone
Is not within our power to prevent.
This life we hold so dear is but a loan—

But brevity of life, which some bemoan,
Should but lend urgency to what is lent,
For life is not a thing that we can own.

Remember what you planted—what has grown?
It comes of what you've done, not what you meant.
This life we hold so dear is but a loan—

You cannot reap what you have never sown!
Waste not another day! Turn and repent,
For life is not a thing that we can own.

Spend life on those you love, or die alone—
And wonder, at the end, where it all went!
This life we hold so dear is but a loan,
For life is not a thing that we can own.

In Favor of Form

by M.P. Lauretta

Today poetic form is ostracized.
It's stifled and suppressed, deemed obsolete;
classed as archaic, stuffy, and effete,
a vestige of the past to be chastised.

Make no mistake, the "advice" is quite prescriptive:
"be modern" and, above all, "just be free"
—though that idea of freedom seems to me
a little overbearing and restrictive.

How long is "modern" modern, anyway?
I ask because they've been at it for ages,
yet after all these years and all their pages,
I still prefer to read Edna Millay.

I too "put chaos into fourteen lines"
—and yes, I *love* it—stuff the philistines!

Foggy Morning Fantasy

by James A. Tweedie

If heaven, as they say, is in the clouds
Then it appears my home and neighborhood
Were raptured in the night. If so, I should
Expect to see streets paved with gold, and crowds
Of saints and martyrs with the heavenly host
Outside my window singing in the mist,
Dignus est Agnus qui occisus est,*
In praise of Father, Son, and Holy Ghost.
Have I arrived on Jordan's distant shore?
Could it be possible that I have been
Translated to the New Jerusalem
Where tears are wiped away and Death's "no more?"
My doorbell rings, but to my great surprise,
A FedEx man… an angel in disguise?

*Latin: "Worthy is the Lamb that was slain" (Revelation 5:12)

What Song Shall I Sing?

by James A. Tweedie

What song shall I sing for a nation divided
By politics, race, economics, and power?
By what sweet refrain shall our nation be guided
Through all that we face in this dark, bitter hour.

Around me the clash of cacophony rages,
The music of dissonance pierces my heart.
For each group and faction creates and engages
Its own sacred anthem that sets it apart.

With everyone marching to different drummers
And bellowing words set to different tunes,
It sounds like ten million insane guitar strummers
All stomping their feet on ten million balloons.

Perhaps I'm naïve to think deep down inside us
A melody lingers that unites us all.
A song we can sing with our neighbor beside us,
With words we once knew and may yet still recall.

A song celebrating the things that unite us;
A song that embraces our hopes and our fears.
A song full of laughter for things that delight us;
A song that remembers our trials and tears.

A song that cries out for the lost and the lonely;
A song that inspires us to give of our best
By saying, "I'll do it!" instead of, "If only…"
A song that reminds us how much we are blessed.

A song that warns not to take freedom for granted;
That justice and liberty wither away

Unless they are constantly pruned and replanted,
Protected, and equally shared every day.

A song which someday we will find ourselves humming
As each of us adds our unique harmony.
A song filled with hope for the years that are coming.
A song of America, home of the free.

For some, such a song would be too controversial.
The media pundits would laugh it to scorn,
And parody it as a TV commercial
For soda, perhaps, both outdated and worn.

Today, some who lead us sing songs of division,
Which glorify anger, despair, and chagrin,
While mocking and pouring contempt on the vision
That celebrates character rather than skin.

Refusing to follow their dire incantation
Is "proof" you're misogynist, racist, or flip.
And any expression of pride in our nation
Is now called "political partisanship."

And then there are those who will try to rename you,
And call you "pathetic," "a failure," or "dumb,"
Attempting to insult, discredit, and shame you,
While squashing you under their opposing thumb.

Express an opinion and someone's offended,
For lines have been drawn in our national sand.
On Fox some won't find their positions defended,
On Facebook and Twitter some find themselves banned.

In spite of it all I will choose to keep singing
Of hope in the midst of our national brawl.
Our bell may be cracked, but the song must keep ringing:
"One nation… with liberty… justice for all."

Commerce of Nations Rendering Homage to Liberty by Edward Moran, 1876, oil on canvas, 95 x 70.5 in.

The Keyhole

by Lynn Michael Martin

Here shut behind an oaken door I stay,
left in a room paneled with times long gone,
and learn to know the passing of the day,
for day and I await the selfsame dawn.
My window faces west, my door is closed
against the east, and since I've seen no sun
except the sun forgotten, I supposed
that I should never see a day begun.
Thus from a child, I was the form of doubt,
and wrote my sonnets to the western lights,
and watched the stars till they had all gone out,
Singing, like sons of dusk, to sleepless nights.
But when the light falls on the keyhole's rim,
I'll sing of dawn, and day shall be my hymn.

Cumæan

by Michael Curtis

Below, beyond the tiles now cavèd down,
Up from the rubbled earth arose a sound
Shrieking in a pitch strung to sting the ear,
Some spirit of a hag command I hear
Of the low, ruined place that was her home,
The Force, the Glory, the Empire, Rome.
"Scan ye now these seven, fully rising hills
From which arose a people bred to kill,
To subjugate all of those around Her,
A people who by will extended order,
Who whipped the wild, conquered by the rod,
Who brought into the world the linking road,
We, the lion's teeth, Mother of the nations."
She spoke in truth, with bare exaggeration.

CUMÆAN: Cumæa is an area of Italy settled by Greeks and associated with an oracle.

Greater Quinquatrus

by Michael Curtis

Grant me fingers nimble as the spider
Who rapidly weaves her fine silken threads;
Let the tight loom and the swift shuttle spread
Woolen patterns as sheer as gossamer.
Kind Minerva, divine artificer,
Grant me accuracy and give me speed,
Allow me to meet my family's need.
Gentle Goddess, please, make me a weaver.
You, mistress of a thousand devices,
Provide your daughter this singular skill
Of web and shuttle, and I shall fulfill
Your pattern. Golden-haired Goddess, bless this
Crafting you wisely ordained me to do,
And I shall give a God-Like art to You.

QUINQUATRUS: an ancient Roman festival sacred to the goddess Minerva, celebrated March 19–23

Horatian

by Michael Curtis

To live the day fully in emptiness
Of song beneath the broadleaved sycamore
Knowing today may not give morrow more
And yet be happy is the classive bliss.
Among the many laureled prayers is this:
"A fertile land with basil near the door,
A kitchen garden flowered for a floor,
An ever-rising spring, a woods sun-kissed,
And wanting neither gold nor fettered ceiling,
Carrara statues crowded to increase;
Instead, unbent to age to be at peace
Among some treasured crafts well placed… breathing."
Turn back the empire to good old ways,
Republican, return the good old days.

CLASSIVE: the practice of human progress through tradition; most often inductive, bottom-up, ascending. As opposed to progressive, which is the belief in human progress through science; most often deductive, top-down, descending.

Prognosis

by C.B. Anderson

Though cosmic looms of kismet or of karma
Determine warp and weft of dread disease,
On earth we face the specter of Big Pharma
Where side-effects outnumber remedies.

What recourse is at hand for those who slipped
Into a coma sans a living will
Or for the bedrid casualties now stripped
Of dignity who've bit the bitter pill?

The herbal and holistic cures no profit
Provide for giant pharmaceutic firms,
But jars arrayed from baseboard to the soffit
On drugstore shelves exploit our fear of germs.

We're made to pay large sums for medicine
That might not work as well as Providence,
Which makes our growing urge to jettison
Prescriptions seem like simple common sense.

South of Eden

by C.B. Anderson

They also serve, who only wait at home
and sow their carrot seed in fertile loam,
in gardens just outside the kitchen door.
In times of need, especially times of war,
agrarian pursuits renew the lease
on life, the comfiture of inner peace,
that many noncombatants thought had gone
away forever.   Written in the dawn,
there is a subtext every gardener knows
by heart: a quaint bucolic ode the rows
of vegetables attest; a summer song
that's manifested in the over-long
endurance daylight shows while staving off
the coming night; and measured lines of soph-
omoric prose, which prove too difficult
for those who've never tasted labor's salt
to comprehend.   It's all about the land,
the land worth fighting for where neighbors stand
together, tethered to a promise made
before the duty owed to clan was laid
in stone, before the right to life was shown
to be a gift impossible to own.
Though seed is sown to meet the creature need
of far tomorrows, nothing's guaranteed.

First published in *Poemeleon*.

Investment Strategies

by C.B. Anderson

At work we studied many charts and graphs
With due attention to the bottom line,
But had we dwelt upon our epitaphs
We would have spent our days decanting wine.

First published in *The Flea*.

The Separate Modalities of Cognition

by C.B. Anderson

Both Aesthetics and Science are studied in vain
If we think with the heart and we feel with the brain.
To observe the distinction 'tween Science and Art,
One should think with the brain and emote with the heart.
When it comes to religion, the nominal goal
Is to focus on God through the lens of the soul.
The conflation of disparate aspects of Light
Will disorder good judgment and lengthen the night.

How We Live Now

by Sally Cook

Forget great men, their truthful ways:
Award them three-day holidays.
The only news is jarring sound—
Peacekeepers moving troops around.

We cherish triviality
And monkeys do as well as we.
Dreaming of going to the stars,
We're strapped and buckled in our cars

But focus on the here and now,
Complacent as some docile cow,
A bovine who's more civilized
Than we. And still, we are surprised

To meet young people who've not read
A single book, yet been to bed
With countless others, in a race
To best their teachers' fall from grace.

We've squeezed the real from everything,
And settled for a high, some bling.
Think of the joy the iPod brings!
Ten thousand songs, yet no one sings.

Drawing with Words

by Sally Cook

The liquid light that poured across that space
Crowned life with golden rays, and gave it grace.
Then later, filled with rosy firelight,
Left embers, glowing on the coldest night.

One chiming clock, one rich red velvet chair
Gave presence to this room; a strange affair.
Those patterns on the rug, which echoed lace,
I reproduced on every parchment space,
Where lines turned into words—a mystery,
I didn't know the meanings for a while.
Till I began to find a writing style.

Some Advice from the Untalented

by Sally Cook

They smugly said I'd never make much money
From playing with my words and making art,
That it would be a waste to spread such honey
So any fool could tear the thing apart.
"Forget it! You have always been contrarian.
There's money to be made and you'd be right
As an accountant, teacher, or librarian.
You've got your back, your feet are good, your sight
Is sure. Why waste it on this silly dream?
A decent mattress beats a lumpy bed
With linens coarse and scratchy; when you scream
You'll muffle it in silken sheets instead.
They only pay an artist when he's dead."

I'm far too mean to die—I'll wait, I said.

I Spent My Youth with Byron and the Bard

by Caleb Winebrenner

I spent my youth with Byron and the Bard,
With Tennyson, the Brownings, and dear Keats—
And full of passions, eager, trying hard
To imitate their lofty, noble feats,
I found it true: the human heart does pump
In echo of the pure iambic line—
And such a card as this I hope may trump
The dealings of my early days, less fine.
With practice, thoughtful minds may hope to pen
A verse as artful, pleasant as 'tis true;
It may well be as yet beyond my ken
To follow right those poets I once knew.
Yet, sonnets in their form will still endure
While verse gives life t' affections known and pure.

Said the Millennial

by Alexander King Ream

Away with what you say we need:
Cars and houses, lawns and seed.
We missed the memo where you sold
A bill of goods, of cost untold.

Autumn Time

by Alexander King Ream

In Autumn time the fag end still
Lingers 'mid November's chill
And finest parts of land and scape
Are found 'mid yards of wine and grape.
Vine and grape then wine's relief;
Drink in Autumn's fine motif.

Sonnet for All Who Follow Me

by Leo Yankevich

Crows and leaves beyond the windowpane,
a cup of steaming coffee on the stool,
my lines reflected in your eyes, which strain
in light as mine once did, the feel of wool
that keeps our stomachs, chests, and shoulders warm
unite us, you now, I who came before.
You wonder how I lived, and ask what harm
beset my age? Floods, earthquakes, famine, war.
Pain transcends the centuries is all
that I can say in speech that has no tenses.
My words part oaks and fly beyond a wall.
They are lamplight reflected in our lenses,
the taste of coffee, cawing in the fall,
the language of the five immortal senses.

EDITOR'S NOTE: The poet Leo Yankevich passed away in December 2018.

Make Christmas a Verb

by Mark F. Stone

For many, the gifts are the be-all and end-all:
the big screen, the tablet, the Barbie and Ken doll.
For me, gifts I get are like ice in the sun.
I cannot recall them. No, not even one.

How did I find a true way to remember
the import of each twenty-fifth of December?
The quest to acquire is an urge one can curb.
The lesson I learned was: make Christmas a verb.

Knock on the door of your neighbors who deal
with aging and loneliness. Bring them a meal.
If you have means and you live in fine fettle,
drop off some greens in that little red kettle.

Visit our vets who are hurt and express
your thanks for their service as they convalesce.
Deliver to others a luminous glow.
The gifts you will cherish are those you bestow.

Two Laws

by Philip Keefe

In this imperfect world, who suffers less:
A good man wrongly jailed with conscience clear?
Another whose low deeds he can't confess
Though from man's laws he nothing has to fear?
The first may sleep quite soundly in his cell,
With physical discomfort he can live;
The miscreant cannot his guilt dispel,
Nor deep down in himself his sins forgive.
For actions can be wrong yet lawful still
And harming others bears this mental price:
That prisons without walls these sinners fill
Who morals and their conscience sacrifice.
    Two sets of laws pertain upon this earth,
      One man's, but moral law much more is worth.

Knowledge as a Mixed Blessing, Part III

by Philip Keefe

That knowledge is benign is oversold,
Its value often proving less than price.
Sometimes we suffer pain from what we're told
And so turns learning's virtue into vice.
Free man must weigh and judge what to believe
As independent thoughts form his own view;
Ideologues wear someone else's weave,
Better minds themselves decide what's true.
On wisdom's path no terminus awaits,
Enlightenment comes not with every stride.
The truth that any prideful person hates:
Sagacity exists where it's denied.
    The man who says that he does little know
    The wiser understanding does he show.

Achievement Surpasses Happiness

by Philip Keefe

So fleet of foot is happiness in life
If we compare it to that laggard care.
With worry, sadly, is existence rife,
Thus peace of mind and true contentment rare.
Yet there are moments when our dark clouds part
And rays of warming sunlight briefly show,
Though beams as these may thaw the coldest heart,
The joy they bring proves just a passing glow.
But man is not a beast with simple needs,
Or satisfied with comfort, food, and drink.
The human mind on each new challenge feeds
And rapture seldom helped his brain to think.
    Euphoria ne'er Seven Wonders made,
      And how their glories much less quickly fade.

Smith on Pollock

by Julian D. Woodruff

It seems the art world all but missed the dart
Hurled 'cross the continent when Hassel Smith
Called Jackson Pollock's paintings "restaurant art";
Or else it put it out of mind forthwith.
We learn, "It's not that Pollock dripped, but how."
How patrons prize his mast'ry of technique—
The practiced toss, the paint mixed to allow
The epic play of line here bold, there sleek.
And yet, Smith's salvo's not to be ignored.
What was the thing that so displeased his eye?
Did Pollock's energy just leave him bored,
Reacting not with "Wow!" but rather, "Why?"
I wonder whether Smith felt in his gut,
"Monumental? Then, monument to what?"

My Daughter Smiles in Her Sleep

by Mark Anthony Signorelli

Some echo maybe of the simple themes
Recurrently unwinding from your toys;
Some analog to listening in dreams
That represents your mother's tranquil voice;

The cadence of my breathing, or the plush,
Recumbent pleasure of your swaddling cloth;
Or else the feeding that has left you flush
And settled to a mute, appropriate sloth;

Whichever of these, the impulse that it loosed
To flit about your organizing brain
Will reify to a vision well adduced
Sometime among your memories that remain;

A kindly apparition, lurking in
The layered shadows of your consciousness—
A haunting and a comfort to you, when
Your years are tried by tedium or duress.

Then you will wonder how a certain scent,
A certain tune, or certain fall of light,
Can, with their own quotidian accidents,
Wake longings tending towards the infinite;

Or why some vague impression half recalled
Out of the general hunger of your youth,
Can leave your unsuspecting soul enthralled
With intimations of another truth;

And from the scattered threads of these perceptions
Your mind will weave a sign of paradise,
Consoling you, in its sublime conception,
Out of a future where its promise lies.

So hackneyed legends tell of mariners' wives
Waiting, in hope, along a monotonous coast
For husbands who already lost their lives
When the schooners that they traded in were lost;

And how they conjured to their minds his form,
His kindly ways, and high gentility,
Who even then was lurching in the storm,
And the fury of an irretrievable sea.

Proverbs for Engraving onto Imperial Monuments

by Daniel Galef

War is the price of freedom. Depths bewilder.
The blow aimed at the beast hits him who shields it.
The sword of Justice best serves him who wields it.
The gibbet's final victim is its builder.
A round coin rolls to him who most deserves it.
A tree outlives its leaves; an age, its fashions.
A carthorse needs its blinders; man, his passions.
The word of Justice best shields him who serves it.
The ardent spirit breaks the firm retort.
Power bears scrutiny like the sun the gaze.
God speaks His queer commands one thousand ways.
The worm awaits. The butterfly is dreaming.
The price of peace is bondage. Chains support.
Persuasion is a proof. Seeing is seeming.

"Proverbs for Engraving" previously published in *Philosophy Now*.

An American in Rome: Sonnets

by Peter Bridges

Headquarters, UN World Food Program

Our fathers sailed in small and leaking boats;
The migrants now march north through deadly sands.
Our mothers in the ghettos sewed cheap coats
And others now replace them from poor lands
Where justice is a website that none sees
And infants' eyes are swarming with black flies
And charcoal's short because there's no more trees
So water can't be boiled and this child dies
Of cholera, who might have grown up great
Else made to be the soldier who at ten
Has learned to cut off hands and how to hate
His world of sad failed states and famines, when
Thin men in sallow camps eat UN rice
And spend their hours at cards and picking lice.

Santa Maria Maggiore

O Lord, Your ways seem hard to understand.
I do not doubt Your majesty when I,
A thing of some few atoms, view the band
Of a billion stars in a clean December sky.
I love the liturgy and pomp and chant
At the Esquiline basilica, on Sunday,
But I can only cry at the cruel and cant
Of some church men when I think back, come Monday,
How the archpriest here presided for so long
In a diocese where pastors buggered boys.
Why would You make that den of sheltered wrong
Your instrument? The very thought destroys
All dreams of good. Old martyrs would decry those Popes
Whose preying priests robbed young boys' pride and hopes.

Via Urbana

The small bells of St. Lawrence sound for seven
In the street where once patricians lived in state
And Peter came to Pudens' to preach heaven
To poor folk in a capital of hate.
I see no walkers, neighbors still asleep,
Just swallows darting happy in high air
With the blackbird singing bold to tell me, "Keep
A true calm heart when times turn foul from fair."
I buy a cappuccino and go sit
By Della Porta's fountain, read the news,
And watch how slow the high old walls get lit
By Father Sun, in a world we may yet lose.
I think of how this old Republic fell;
Our own across the sea is far from well.

PUDENS: Roman senator visited in his home by Saint Peter
Image: *Basilica di Santa Maria Maggiore* by Giuseppe Vasi, 1747

Victus

*a response to William Ernest Henley's poem "Invictus,"
from which the first two lines of the final stanza are taken*

by Luke Hahn, high school poet

Dry chatter of dry souls dies out,
Beleaguered by the eastern wind,
When this world's chaff is blown about:
The chaff of every soul that sinned.

Their tongues grow swollen in their throats,
Numb to the bitter gall of death;
So, boldly do they board the boats
That bear man o'er the final breath!

But the wind rises in those sails
And topples them into the Pit,
Surrounded by their pangs and wails:
The fruit sown by their worldly grit.

"It matters not how strait the gate,
How charged with punishments the scroll,"
The Lord is master of my fate:
The captain of my conquered soul.

Keeping the Door

by James Sale

Ant hordes scurried in purposeful files;
Angry, alert, full to demonic marching:
They came in batteries to batter:
    But I kept the door.

Worms twisted achingly upwards into wiles
Of air and ever coiled most arching
On pathways which would be straighter, later;
    But I kept the door.

Flies swarmed, furtive, across cow-spattered piles
Of filth scenting another kind of charging
On which they could clamber, puke, lather;
    But I kept the door.

Butterflies in legions, larvae-bursting smiles,
All innocent as green is in Spring's urging—
So did pity move me more, and rather.
    Still I kept the door.

Displaced: The Trail of Tears

by Janice Canerdy

As rain falls hard and soaks the ground
and thunder roars its mighty sound,
so tears of the displaced may fall,
their cries bespeaking dearth and pall.

The Deep South tribes of long ago
were forced to forge a trail of woe,
of death and want, with goods so small,
their cries bespeaking dearth and pall.

The Cherokees were brought to tears
when forced from land they'd held for years,
no longer standing strong and tall,
their cries bespeaking dearth and pall.

The rugged journey thousands made
to Westward land should never fade
from memory. We must recall
their cries bespeaking dearth and pall.

VII. NARRATIVES

Not an Idle Minute by Heide Presse, 2019, oil on linen, 30 x 20 in. (HeidePresse.com)

The Three Graces in the Trinket Shop

Aglaia, Euphrosyne, Thalia

by Joseph S. Salemi

I find them there, no longer young,
Though neatly dressed and well preserved:
Three sisters in the trinket shop—
Polite and helpful, but reserved.

They guide me through their small boutique
Of jewelry, knickknacks, souvenirs;
Of statuettes and china plates;
Of teacups, lamps, and chandeliers;

Daguerreotypes and candlesticks;
Framed engravings, rosaries;
Liqueur glasses, beaded shawls;
Old postcards from the Tuileries.

I wonder at their careful speech—
The reticence and cryptic air
With which they describe every piece,
As chill as penitential prayer.

I ask to see the cameos
(Mostly profiles carved in shell)
And notice, in the crowded case,
Un délicat, exceptionnel:

Aglaia, Euphrosyne,
Thalia veiled in gauzy stuff,
On tiptoe as they spin like leaves
Swept upwards by a zephyr's puff.

The Charites or Gratiae—
Three twirling maids whose dance delights.
They follow Aphrodite's steps
And serve as her attendant sprites.

So says one sister when I ask—
The others smile but seem remote
As if they thought how well the jewel
Would grace some shell-pink female throat

But not their own. No longer theirs
The gifts of agile charm and glow.
Three sisters in a trinket shop
Whose movements are precise and slow

Can only keep youth's girlish dance
Preserved within a locked display
Where memory might—now and then—
Recall a more ungoverned day.

Virgin Annunciate or *The Annunciation* by Antonello da Messina, 1475, oil on panel, 17.7 x 13.5 in. Currently located in Palermo, Italy.

On Antonello Da Messina's
The Annunciation

by Joseph S. Salemi

Palermo's great basilica is still—
All prayers are tongueless for a lonely hour.
Here high and holy silence can be breathed
Like incense from the smoking thuribles
Swung by acolytes at solemn mass.

Antonello's Virgin turns her eyes
Ever so gently to one side. Perhaps
The sacristan has shuffled into view
To snuff a candle, or replace dried blooms
In the small vase atop her votive shrine.

Robed in heavy blue, she cannot move
Her head more than a barely noticed notch,
Her pearl-pure skin enshrouded in a weight
Of ultramarine, as ponderously dark
As far-off mountains when the vespers ring.

Nevertheless, she lifts a sculpted hand
(So perfect in its shape and comeliness
That God Himself might envy its chaste form)
And holds it forth in admonition to
Whatever has disturbed her solitude.

The angel of annunciation? No:
Her cool composure's quite untouched by fear
Or marvel at a preternatural light—
Her face shows brief distraction from her thoughts
Caused by some human presence, nothing more.

NARRATIVES - JOURNAL VIII

The sacristan most likely, for he comes
On no fixed schedule, and his heavy tread
Breaks the cathedral's silence, while his gown
Swishes along the foot-smooth slabs of stone
That pave the aisle up to the Virgin's niche.

Or else he is too stealthy in his steps—
His sudden, startling presence may have irked
Our Lady, who in pure Sicilian says
Fa scrusciu, pregu, quann' intrati ccà!
(Make some stir, please, when you enter here!)

She uses arch *intrati*, a prim verb
With high-class connotations that recall
Dante's *Inferno* and its fabled gate;
Out in the street you would have heard *trasiti*—
But after all, she is the Holy Virgin.

Chastened by Our Lady's soft reproach
The sacristan—done trimming candle wicks—
Gathers his gown and tiptoes quietly
Back to his cloister, where he meditates
On Satan as the Father of All Noise.

In any case, strict silence falls anew
After the man's departure, and remains
Until devotions fill the spacious church.
Some simple souls kneel at the altar rail
To whisper decades of their rosaries

But when they reach the mystery of how
A messenger came to a humble girl
To tell what would befall her, even they
Know this face too wise and self-possessed
For God's own sovereign voice to disconcert.

From *Skirmishes*, Pivot Press, 2010.

Taxi from Mohonk

by James Sale

The taxi driver took us down
From great Mohonk, New Paltz and such;
And every mile we got to touch
We felt the pull of New York town.

And chatting in our easy way—
He black, me white, what difference then?
Only as humans, two grown men,
We both outlined our lives today.

What did it mean to be a Yank?
To be a Brit so far from home?
Each saw the other as his own:
Before God, true—there is no rank.

Then he expressed his great surprise:
I was the first Brit in his cab
He'd ever met, who'd ever had
Belief One strong upheld the skies.

Leonidas

the Spartan king at the Pass of Thermopylae, 480 B.C.

by Evan Mantyk

Eyes narrow as the pure-blood king looks through
The jagged cliffs to where the Persians march
Around to do soon what they've yearned to do:
Enclose the Greeks within a fatal arch.

He hears their footsteps counting down the time
To when his far, far smaller force is trapped
Then slaughtered cold thanks to some traitor's crime.
Resolved, he simply speaks and all are rapt:

"You other Greeks must quickly flee from here
To live and fight for Greece another day,
But as for us three hundred it is clear:
Our orders have not changed, therefore we stay."

And thus the noble Spartans died yet won;
Their foes' morale was crushed—they were outdone.

Right to Left

a poem of political viewpoint

by Tony L. Damigo

While passing through the town-hall square,
   I came across a stump.
I thought 'twas perfect for debate,
   so on it, I did jump.

While calling to my friends and peers,
   I feared that I was dead!
A stone the size of half my fist
   came flying at my head.

I dodged the rock and found myself
   still standing on the stump.
Then felt a pain upside my head,
   and fell with a loud thump!

The opposition claimed that I
   was not a passive man.
He swore I was not tolerant;
   a blight upon the land!

He twisted words said in my past;
   spoke of worthless people.
He fanned the flames of discontent,
   and claimed that I was evil.

He vowed that he would win this race,
   and make a better world.
And stood there with another rock
   ready to be hurled!

The Old Man Goes to Bed

to Rogelio

by Martin Rizley

The corner house has one light lit
As now the clock strikes one.
The winter moon ascends to sit
Where lately sat the sun;
From high up in the clear night sky
It sheds cold light upon
The sleeping town, where most now lie
Like dead men till the dawn.

Inside, the old man strives to keep
His vigil by the fire,
But heavy eyelids, charged with sleep,
Now bid him to retire.
He sets his violin aside
And rises to his feet
To leave, like the withdrawing tide,
This isle of light and heat.

He stands beside the hearth awhile
And with a poker stirs
A few bright embers, which the pile
Of ash swiftly inters.
Outside, a lone dog barks his brute
Complaints to all around,
But this old man, resigned and mute,
Makes not the slightest sound.

He turns an old key in the latch
And checks the whole house well,
Just like a chick, about to hatch
Turns round inside its shell.

Then, having stopped to set the clock,
Through darkened halls he winds;
And having checked the back door lock,
And having drawn the blinds,

He takes one long and pensive look
At where his heart's desire
Would sweetly sit and read a book
Beside a roaring fire.
But now the flames have all died out—
The ash lies cold tonight—
So with one final look about,
He switches off the light.

Beside his bed, he strips and seems
A ghost beside a tomb
Bathed in the light of spectral beams
That shine into his room.
Once tucked beneath his quilt so warm
The old man lies content,
And gazes on a lovely form,
So round and eloquent—

The silent moon, that rides on high,
Godiva-like, both nude
And radiant in the empty sky,
Sublime in solitude;
Beholding, as it were, his twin,
The old man shuts his eyes,
And soon, the two will fade from view
And sink in the sunrise.

The Pain of Foreign Occupation

a true story

by Leo Zoutewelle

The land lay naked under hobnailed boots
Of German occupiers in The Hague.
The Blitzkrieg had commenced with parachutes
And covered sedate Holland like a plague.

That's how the war began, there in the west;
First Rotterdam was savagely destroyed,
A terrible example for the rest
If quick surrender was not now employed.

The queen, expatriated to Great Britain,
Thus did not have a real choice anymore
And so the bitter truce was quickly written,
But even then, the men breathed "nevermore!"

***

A little boy was playing with his trike,
Safe on his sidewalk, riding up and down
When 'cross the street a soldier of the Reich
Emerged, sat down nearby and showed a frown.

He called the boy, who stared at him: "Come here,
Come, little man and sit with me a spell."
He took him up and, "what's your name, my dear?"
"My name's Jerome, and I can spell it well."

"You're clever; what a pretty name, 'Jerome';
I have a little boy at home like you.
His name is Klaus." *"But where then is your home?"*
"In Hamburg, son, you'd love our Hamburg stew!"

"But why then are you here?" The soldier stalled...
"Well, I'm a soldier and I have to do
That which my gen'ral ordered when he called."
"What did he order when he called for you?"

"Uh, well... He told me to come here, with gift...
say 'hey' to you, be nice and never frown..."
"That was real nice of him!" The soldier sniffed
And looked red-faced, a little like a clown.

"Well, I must go now, I enjoyed our talk;
Perhaps we'll meet again another day."
He gently put the boy down on the walk;
Not looking back, he dragged the chair away.

Jerome saw him go back inside, then turned
And crossed the street to go and find his mom
Who would, he thought, by now be well concerned.
He found her teary-eyed, but strangely calm.

She'd seen the whole event but didn't act:
She understood the German's deference
And counted on her son's instinctive tact,
Which was much to her thoughtful preference.

So when Jerome was well tucked in his bed
He thought again, *"Why did he really come?*
He didn't come to be with me instead
Of going to his own son's cozy home?"

Then sleepily he mused, *"I wish he'd brought*
His son along so I could play with him,"
But then he did succumb with that one thought.
And all the thoughts of men with guns turned dim.

NARRATIVES - JOURNAL VIII

Rain

by James Preston Pack, high school poet

Rain, lapping at the windows fast,
falls cold and ceaseless, painting lines
of marble on the silvered glass
while clouds cast dark and thunder whines;
but these walls will not let it pass
and through a cloud-gap sunlight shines.

I watch it from the darkened room,
for I am waiting for my doom.

As I sling off my coat, I sit,
watch fire lighting the dark den,
as shadows, dancing, candle-lit,
crawl closer and turn into men
who swarm around me; now one sits
and eyes me, cornered beast, here penned.

I look away, ashamed, and think
what had been wrought by debt and drink.

He looks me over, wondering
what impulses of anger can
provoke such deeds, such awful things—
he asks me, knowing, why I ran,
and hears the truth; I cannot sing
my lies: I say I killed a man.

He owed me ten, he thought it five,
I could not leave a cheat alive.

His sigh clouds up against the glass
and mingles with the droplets there,
still falling, as if this young lass
had never killed, or never shared

her deed with others. Then he asks—
why had I laid my actions bare.

He asks me why I thought to kill
to right a debt, to pay a bill.

Why had I killed?—it was not right
to ask me that, I told the man;
there is no cause, I said, to fight,
to kill, make war, but that we can:
we must, I fear, make right by might,
it is our kills that help us stand.

The falling rain makes dark the room;
I am still waiting for my doom.

Saint Francis and the Wolf of Gubbio

by Alan Sugar

It seemed a wolf had terrorized the town.
Well, isn't that what wolves are wont to do?
The people said, "Say, put that wild thing down."
"Or else, instead, give it a talking to."
A man named Francis had a special way
of speaking with the creatures of the wood.
He was the Doc Dolittle of his day.
And all in nature knew that he was good.
Approaching near and fearing not its jaw,
he whispered to the wolf without restraint.
On hearing this, the wolf held out a paw
and winked as if to say, "You are a saint."
The people then befriended it. What's more—
they welcomed man and beast at every door.

Icarus' Fall at College

by Ron L. Hodges

Prologue

Dear reader, surely, you must think,
    "What could be taught to us
That we haven't already learned
    Of mythic Icarus?
"His plunge is clearly a warning—
    Don't be consumed with pride—
Which is the classical insight
    On how Icarus died.
"And we know the modern readings,
    Those that rewrite the script
From the tale of a careless boy
    To one heroic trip."
So, of the Icarus legend,
    You're sure all has been said,
Yet if you'll patiently listen,
    I'll weave another thread.

I.

Yes, it was the classical case
    Of teenage life, downbeat;
Young Icarus seemed doomed to die
    In his hometown of Crete.
He longed to reach a different shore,
    Where grew a fruitful knowledge,
And knew escape was his to win
    Through getting into college.
Plus, he had heard another myth
    Of how collegiate life
Would vivify the shriveled mind
    With salutary strife.
His father, Daedalus, agreed
    To send him on his way;

For Daedalus the architect,
    College seemed a wise foray.
Yet, he knew he must prepare him
    For dangers he would face;
While college could exalt his mind,
    It also might abase:
"My dear son, I must now warn you,
    Loose feelings clog the sight,
And there are those who melt the heart
    To commandeer your flight;
"On your journey, be collected—
    Don't let passions get too high—
For when one has lost perspective,
    His steering goes awry."
Icarus, in truth, was puzzled;
    This seemed a silly fear;
In a place of so much sunlight,
    Could sight just disappear?

II.

Oh, Icarus was euphoric
    On that first day of class—
His vista shined so luminous
    Swept by the airy mass!
Like a bird floats on the current,
    He sailed into the hall,
Where the hope of proffered wisdom
    Was like a siren's call.
Young Icarus sat and waited
    For new life to begin;
As he scanned the other faces,
    He felt amongst his kin.
It was then the teacher entered,
    Trailed by a ponytail.
He sported a graying goatee
    Specked by a shard of kale.
The wise man began to lecture,
    His words a burning sun;

Icarus was drawn by its theme:
 Privilege and oppression.
Though the substance of the message
 Filled Icarus with shame,
This loathing for his Grecian skin
 Induced a righteous aim.
Emotion waxed inside his soul,
 Casting all thoughts aside.
It was as if his father's words
 Were swept off by the tide.

III.

Each lecture the boy attended
 Was like a scroll unfurled,
On which oracles had written
 How hearts could save the world.
Soon, he joined a campus movement—
 "The Suns of Equity"—
Whereby he hoped to stand upon
 The crux of history.
They pondered righteous acts to do
 While eating Lotus plant,
And concluded nightly meetings
 With a two-minute chant.
Then, one night, they got specific—
 An enemy would soon arrive—
Who planned to air his hateful views,
 And threaten their museful hive.
"Listen to what this bigot wrote,"
 Their angry leader spat;
"He cannot be allowed to speak—
 Just listen to this rat!"
"'The greatest of inequities?'"
 Their enraged leader read,
"'Making unequal things equal!'"—
 They cried, "We'll have his head!"
So, they painted some protest signs,
 Blazing with golden words,

And to symbolize true freedom,
    They dressed like Mockingbirds.

IV.

Like in a play by Sophocles,
    The fateful day had come,
When the crash of misplaced passion
    Begets a tragic sum.
They entered the bright lecture room,
    Icarus and his flock;
When the speaker reached his lectern,
    They each began to squawk,
And shook their signs and flapped their wings,
    As if tossed in a storm,
So earnest were they not to grant
    This speaker a platform.
The bearded speaker looked in shock
    At this flapping, birdbrained crew;
Though most there wanted him to speak,
    Those birds had staged a coup.
Security stood on the side,
    Not wanting to engage,
But some stood up to force them out,
    Which filled the birds with rage!
The protest leader grabbed his club,
    Swung at approaching heads,
And others nearby joined the fray,
    As a sudden ripple spreads.
For a moment, Icarus heard
    His father's farewell words,
Yet soon drowned in that angry sea,
    Which pulled his heart onwards.
The bright room throbbed under the lights;
    They pressed against his back
Like sunshine on a noonday beach,
    Compelling his attack.
Icarus' veins throbbed in his head
    As he blindly flailed his fists;

It was as if his sovereign soul
     Had now ceased to exist.
Suddenly, struck hard by something,
     The young protester fell;
And when, later, he awakened,
     He lay in a prison cell!

V.

No one had died, but Icarus
     Was charged with battery,
And then he was expelled from school,
     Despite his tearful plea.
So Icarus returned to Crete,
     Beggared, but unashamed;
For the tragic fall he'd suffered,
     The bourgeoisie he blamed.
Yet he couldn't live with father,
     A rightist, he now knew;
He would crash with the Minotaur
     And ponder what to do.
He worked as a mere barista,
     But knew he was no slouch,
For Icarus would change the world
     From his friend's sleeper couch.

Epilogue

Ah, there you are, gentle reader,
     A new spin on the tale,
Which shows that no hubris alone
     Caused Icarus to fail.
The truth is it was a symptom
     Born of a captured mind—
When one feels his cause is holy,
     He's passionately blind.
The emotions must be balanced
     By factual content,

And grounded with humble reason—
 That's what Daedalus had meant.
So, heed the words of Daedalus
 Lest the passions get too high,
For then you will lose your perspective,
 And tumble from the sky.

The Fall of Icarus by Jacob Peter Gowy, c. 1635,
oil on canvas, 76.6 x 70.8 in.

At Königstein Festung

by Gleb Zavlanov

Within the shadow of the fortress wall,
I stand agape; such gross, exquisite scale.
My bulging eyes attempt to take in all
But sadly, unsurprisingly, they fail.
Hot inspiration spikes; aroused, I call,
"Wake up, you bricks, speak up, recount your tale."
I push my ear against their rugged stone;
They chant their story to my ear alone:

The piercing clink of hammer, rock and nail,
The groans of workers straining in the heat,
Unfalteringly slaving through harsh hail,
Rough rain, sharp snow, stark sun, and slicing sleet,
Until, a thing no army could assail,
It stands, impregnable, a noble feat;
The ingenuity of engineers
To last as strong as ever through the years.

I wander up the stairs, amazed, upbeat,
My mounting spirit just about to burst
From fresh excitement, knowing that my feet
Here, through these ancient halls, are not the first,
That centuries saw a million soles beat
This very floor in times of best and worst.
I trace those soles up to a post and draw
A panting breath of wonder, joy, and awe.

NARRATIVES - JOURNAL VIII

A mystifying landscape beams and broods.
Arranged in likeness of a grisly spine,
A dark and daunting mountain range protrudes
Through looming colonnades of spruce and pine
Whose misty groves once crawled with multitudes
That dared to test the might of Königstein,
That plotted months in vengeful secrecy
Amid dense forest tenebrosity.

Now, I'm no longer me, no longer here,
No longer now, but cast in centuries back,
A stationed sentry, gripping on his spear
With paling knuckles, eyeing country track,
Convinced, lips chewed, that armies will appear
From foggy woods to mount the huge attack.
I picture them, upon the rising sun,
In roaring swarms, rush, glinting weapons drawn.

Beset with thirst, I venture to our well,
Grown thick with vine and oozing watercress,
Where, with deep panting, quaffing slurps, I quell
My cracking thirst on nature's blessedness,
Then stare, amazed, at how it worms to Hell,
No point untouched by Saxon edifice,
When, suddenly, with glorious alarm,
Bells clamor, warning of approaching harm.

I scramble to my parapet, hand taut
Upon my spear, heart pounding in my chest,
And, petrified, gape at the juggernaut
Advancing, loud with rancorous unrest.
I feel my body jitter, head grow hot.
I kiss my cross with frightened, fervent zest,
Prepared to shed my honorable blood
For Saxon kings, for Saxony, for God.

NARRATIVES - JOURNAL VIII

"Aim, fire!" Arrows hiss like locust hordes,
An ecstasy of scrambling horror peaks.
The shrilly chafing shimmer of drawn swords
Drains every speck of color from my cheeks.
My twisted tongue flops through a thousand words
And frantic, frothing phrases as it seeks
To clump whatever hasty orison
My terror-stricken soul can draw upon.

Shouts, yells, and bangs, demented whimpering.
I dizzy from the nauseating dread.
Men scream, blood pours, shields bang, flames rage, swords swing.
I feel a fainting flitter in my head.
Then, suddenly, a vicious, snapping sting
Zips through my neck. My vision swells with red.
I reel, eyes writhing, darting up to God,
Then, wheezing, rasping, drop, choked up on blood.

I start from that unsettling dream, cold sweat
Pearled on my brow, fear tensing on my face,
Transported from that fateful parapet
Back to my time, my body, and my place.
I look out at the villages, afret
With modern life's smooth, mechanistic pace,
Hosts of belligerent and zealous knights
Replaced with cars and soothing neon lights.

The Turkey Vulture

after Edgar Allan Poe's "The Raven"

by Anna J. Arredondo

Years ago—I still remember: final Thursday in November,
I was in my kitchen cooking food to rival feasts of yore;
To and fro sashaying, hopping, slicing, dicing, mincing, chopping,
Dish by dish—no time for stopping, for so daunting was the chore:
Playing hostess for Thanksgiving—such a monumental chore
    I had never faced before.

Busying myself with basting, reading recipes, and tasting,
I was filled with gratitude for all the things that I adore.
Blithely counting every blessing, I prepared some cornbread dressing,
Barely wond'ring, never guessing what the future had in store;
Thankful for both past and present, what the future had in store
    On this day I could ignore.

When at last I'd finished baking, how my lower back was aching!
Yet my heart was filled with gladness, and my face a smile wore:
After hours of preparation, it was time for celebration,
And with great anticipation I received folks at the door;
Jubilant anticipation as I opened wide the door
    To the guests I'd labored for.

Round the table, bright and perky, we all dined on roasted turkey,
Squash, potatoes, stuffing, gravy, bread, and casseroles galore.
Soon our appetites were slowing; nonetheless we kept on going,
In our swelling bellies stowing two desserts, or three, or four—
So much succulent dessert, we had to eat, like, three or four,
    Till our stomachs were quite sore.

NARRATIVES - JOURNAL VIII

Then all those who still were able helped me—clearing off the table,
Bringing back into the kitchen ample leftovers to store.
Next: what could be fitter closing than to celebrate by dozing?
Soon the guests were all reposing on the sofas and the floor,
Nodding, napping, sweetly dreaming on the sofas and the floor.
    Who could ever ask for more?

This I pondered, reminiscing: not one thing desired was missing;
Such abundance chased away the slightest thought of being poor.
Suddenly, I had the notion there was something still in motion
'Mid the softly slumbering ocean and its low collective roar;
Yes, I thought I'd heard a noise above the low collective roar
    That was not just one more snore.

Then—most clearly—something rustled; to my feet I leapt and hustled
(Or I tried to hustle, rather, dodging dreamers on the floor)
To the kitchen, quickly bounding, stopping short with heart
    a-pounding
When I spied the most astounding sight before my icebox door:
An enormous turkey vulture tugging at my icebox door
    Was the sound I'd heard before.

Ah, this bird was sure no craven (out-sized any crow or raven
That had ever fluttered through the grandest poetry of yore)—
Wasting not a moment perching, awkwardly the thing was lurching
Through my kitchen, bobbing, searching for some carcasses to score;
Just a bold, brash buzzard seeking some fresh carcasses to score—
    Or, perhaps, a petit four?

Bothered by this home invasion; loath to let it spoil th' occasion—
Such were my conflicting feelings as I viewed the brutish boor.
So I mustered up some caring, genuine, unselfish sharing
For this feathered fowl, whose daring search had brought it to implore;
This vile vulture, which had come some light refreshment to
    implore—
    How could I his plight ignore?

There he stood, his feathers puffing, watching as I served him stuffing,
Bones, and giblets heaped together (to resemble natural gore),
And, when I had finished styling thus the food that I was piling,
I could swear the bird was smiling as he ravenously tore—
With a shocking lack of manners—through those turkey scraps he tore.
    Then that beast said, "Gimme more!"

"Please and thank you, bird," I grumbled, and some more choice words I mumbled,
But the creature, quite unflustered, could not grasp why I was sore.
Then, ere I had finished scolding, that large vulture, wings unfolding,
Offered me what he'd been holding—dumped it, rather, on the floor:
Ads and flyers, discounts, coupons, scattered there upon my floor
    With their message: Gimme more!

Such obnoxious advertising on this day was most surprising
(This day, set apart for stating all that we are thankful for);
Every miracle of science, every gadget and appliance,
Dazzling in their defiance of my gladness heretofore;
Countless items challenging the gladness I had heretofore,
    Whisp'ring to me, "Gimme more."

Shocked into dissatisfaction (yet ashamed of my reaction),
Paralyzed, I stood and ogled ads from every shop and store,
Till a drowsy guest, half-waking from the nap that she was taking,
Spoke, the wretched silence breaking—spoke the words that could restore;
Though she murmured, still half-sleeping, yet my sense she could restore—
    "Thanks," she sighed, "I need no more"—

Uttered out of peaceful dreaming, welcome words, like beacons, beaming,
Shining, scattering the darkness of the greed I so abhor.
"This is more than I can swallow: having things, but feeling hollow.
Out they go, and you will follow!" said I, as each ad I tore—
Each and every advertisement littering my floor I tore.
    Still the bird croaked, "Gimme MORE!"

"Beastly bird!" Now I was yelling, "I don't want a thing you're selling.
I'm quite satisfied, I tell you; I am happy to the core!
All this junk, although you love it, I am in no mood to covet—
You can take your greed and shove it! You're becoming quite a bore."
And that rude, red-headed buzzard (who was really quite a bore)
    Yet protested, "Gimme more!"

"Liar," howled I, "foul deceiver!" and I wildly waved my cleaver,
"Take your greedy 'gimme' gospel to some far-off, distant shore.
I am through with being bullied! Leave my happiness unsullied,
Disappear from my life fully—darken nevermore my door.
Take your greed from out my house, and take yourself out through my door;
    Bring your 'gimme more' no more!"

Only thus—with threats and shouting, and some fierce invective spouting—
Did I manage to escort the feathered felon out the door.
Rid of his repulsive squealing, my attention turned to healing
And recovering the feeling of contentment from before—
All the peace and satisfaction that was filling me before
    He first grunted, "Gimme more."

Off he flew into the morrow, luring folks to spend and borrow,
So this holiday I merely nearly managed to restore:
Ever since—it's most appalling—once a year the bird comes calling,
And its flight on Friday falling clouds the day we're thankful for—
Yes, its evil shadow falling back on all we're thankful for
    Shall be lifted—nevermore.

VIII. TRANSLATIONS

The Fountain of the Tritons in the Island Garden, Aranjuez
by Diego Rodríguez de Silva y Velázquez, 1657,
oil on canvas, 97.6 x 87.7 in.

Despedida al Real Sitio de Aranjuez

Fértiles bosques de Aranjuez florido,
por donde se desliza el Tajo undoso;
prado de mil colores guarnecido,
do siempre halló mi corazón reposo;
felices avecillas, que a mi oído
halagabais con canto melodioso,
voy a dejaros ya; pero mi acento
antes os mostrará mi sentimiento.

En vuestras agradables espesuras
a mi voz inspiró naturaleza;
en ellas olvidé las amarguras
de mi suerte cruel; vuestra belleza,
mi corazón llenando de dulzuras,
ha cambiado en placeres mi tristeza;
y en vuestro mudo y plácido sosiego
desprecié altiva el amoroso fuego.

Esta tranquilidad, que ha recobrado
en vuestra soledad el alma mía;
la razón, que mi espíritu ha elevado,
para lograr vencer la suerte impía;
y en fin, el tierno metro que ha inspirado
a mi genio la dulce poesía;
a ti lo debo, sitio delicioso,
donde mi corazón fue venturoso.

TRANSLATIONS - JOURNAL VIII

Farewell to the Royal Gardens at Aranjuez

by María Rosa Gálvez de Cabrera of Spain (1768–1806)
from Spanish by Martin Hill Ortiz

Aranjuez: forest, rich with flowers,
Through which the tangled Tajo glides,
Within your thousand brilliant colors
A meadow where my heart resides.
And how your songbirds flattered me!
I'd swear they'd sung for me alone.
I offer them this melody:
A poem, my own peculiar tone.

Within the pleasance of your trees
I came upon my earthy voice,
Abandoning the rasp and wheeze
Of once cruel luck. My heart rejoiced
In your allure and through your charms,
I found my sorrows turned to sighs.
In solace, in your cradling arms:
The fire of love I'd once despised.

Your placidness restored my soul—
You, too, possessed a lonely weight.
Our spirits joined, our spirits whole,
Rose up to conquer cursèd fate.
You are this verse's tender meter,
The tingle in my clever brain.
I owe you all, no joy is sweeter
Than that I knew in your domain.

A Dios quedad, llanuras agradables,
montes, jardines, selvas y cascadas;
mientras respire, me seréis amables,
pues me dieron alivio estas moradas:
el sosiego y la paz, inestimables
tesoros de las horas ya pasadas,
vivan siempre y habiten vuestro seno,
de mil placeres y hermosura lleno.

Quédate a Dios, oh gruta deliciosa,
donde su curso unió Tajo y Jarama;
nunca el verdor de tu arboleda hermosa
destruya el sol con ardorosa llama:
vuestra corriente bañe silenciosa
del verde prado la naciente grama;
y en su llanura las pintadas flores
den al suelo esplendor y al viento olores.

En tu elogio, Aranjuez, se oirán en tanto
los olvidados ecos de mi lira,
sin que la vanidad mueva mi canto,
pues es la gratitud la que me inspira:
aquí cesó la causa de mi llanto;
de mi persecución calmó la ira;
y pues del hado aquí logré victoria,
siempre me será grata tu memoria.

The Lord sustains your pleasant fields,
Your thickets, gardens, and cascades.
With bracing breaths your mercy yields
Release. I found within your glades
A calmness. Peace, your priceless treasure,
Persists beyond our coupled hours.
Your bosom holds a thousand pleasures,
And amorous, seducing powers.

The Lord has placed a grotto where
The Tajo and Jarama meet.
Your verdant groves have deigned to spare
The stolid sun from ardent heat.
The silent river currents nourish
The meadowlands where grasses sway.
The plains where painted flowers flourish
Suffuse the winds with their bouquets.

Aranjuez, there, my praise remains,
Though echoes of my song shall dwindle
Without my voice to sing refrains.
Such gratitude have you enkindled:
You quelled the causes of my wailing,
The wrath-filled torments I once knew.
I triumphed, and, in so prevailing,
I joyously remember you.

Untitled French Original

Nature ne fait rien
De dissolucion,
Se ce n'est par moien,
Nature ne fait rien;
Quand le naturien
Y met solucion,
Nature ne fait rien
De dissolucion.

Nature ne fait rien
Que par comandement
Du roy celestien,
Qui la fist proprement
Et donna sentement
De bonne intencion,
Non pas entendement
De dissolucion.

Se ce n'est par moyen
D'aucun qui folement
Preingne divers maintien
En son esbatement,
Ou Nature ne sent
En sa condition
Aucun atouchement
De dissolucion.

Understanding Nature

by Jean Froissart (c.1335–c.1410)
from French by Margaret Coats

    Nature fashions nothing
    By random evolution;
    Without real causes prompting
    Nature fashions nothing.
    Though scholars rant in plotting
    Against her constitution,
    Nature fashions nothing
    By random evolution.

    Nature fashions nothing
    Except as God created,
    In wisdom once allotting
    The forms she propagated;
    To her He delegated
    Sure means of distribution;
    She is not animated
    By random evolution.

    Without real causes prompting,
    Researchers permeated
    By ignorance besotting
    Trust theories outdated,
    But Nature has restated
    That chance is no solution,
    And time is overrated
    By random evolution.

Quant le naturien
Bien congnoisant entent
Parler contre le bien
De Nature, il ne tent
Qu'a honneur et briefment
Y met solucion,
Et l'escuse humblement
De dissolucion.

The Poem of the Soul — Divine Genesis by Louis Janmot,
19th century, oil on canvas, 44.3 x 56.3 in.

Though scholars rant in plotting
Their unsubstantiated
Denials when confronting
What Nature legislated,
Such science fabricated
Against her constitution
Discredits them, deflated
By random evolution.

TRANSLATOR'S NOTES: 1.) "Understanding Nature" by Jean (or Jehan) Froissart is translated not very literally but as far as possible in the original form, with its elaborate repetition and rhyme scheme.
2.) Yes, the medieval author defies evolution. He calls it "dissolution," meaning "disorder," and thereby denouncing the idea of creation from chaos. He would also reject another concept known in his time, that life can come from nonliving matter, such as rotting wood that in "dissolution" seems to produce maggots. If he knew of it, he would affirm the second law of thermodynamics, which states that disorder in natural systems always increases, and thus cannot give rise to more complex order in nature, no matter how much time there is for chance to operate.

Untitled French Original

Amours est le pain qui repaist
Par grace les cuers familleux;
Amours est le vin qui tant plaist,
Amours et le pain qui repaist.
Amours est le conseil tout prest
A refraindre les merveilleux;
Amours est le pain qui repaist
Par grace les cuers familleux.

Amours est le pain qui repaist
Le cuer de creature humaine;
Amours est la clef et l'arrest
Qui tient les cuers en son demaine;
Amours les bons cuers à bien maine;
Amours est le grain vertueux
Qui repaist de manne mondaine
Par grace les cuers familleux.

Amours est le vin qui tant plaist,
Odourant souef comme graine,
Amours scet bien comment il est
A ses gens et lesquels ont paine;
Amours scet qui en vain se paine,
Amours est le fruit gracieux
Qui raemplist, oudoure, alaine
Par grace les cuers familleux.

Amours est le conseil tout prest
A conseiller honnour haultaine;
Amours donne, sans faire prest,
Ses biens par vertu souveraine;
Amours est frain et bride saine
A refraindre les merveilleux,
Et qui assouage et ramaine
Par grace les cuers familleux.

True Likeness

by Jean Froissart (c.1335–c.1410), from French by Margaret Coats

Love is the bread that nourishes
A family's hearts with honeyed grace;
Love is the wine a home relishes,
Love is the bread that nourishes,
Love is the counsel that banishes
Contrary claims when kindred embrace;
Love is the bread that nourishes
A family's hearts with honeyed grace.

Love is the bread that nourishes
Health in pure hearts, and spiritual gain;
Love is the key that furnishes
Freedom and friendship in duty's domain;
Love shows kind hearts how virtues reign;
Love is the consecrated space
Where banquets of manna entertain
A family's hearts with honeyed grace.

Love is the wine a home relishes,
Sweetening lives austere or plain;
Love understands and cherishes
Those of his own who suffer pain;
Love soothes the troubles that vex life in vain.
Love is the fruit whose flavor can brace
Courage in households ready to train
A family's hearts with honeyed grace.

Love is the counsel that banishes
Anger from honor's noble terrain;
Love in itself accomplishes
Anything gentle words ordain.
Love is a bridle, quick to restrain
Contrary claims when kindred embrace,
Offering comforts fit to sustain
A family's hearts with honeyed grace.

Aquila et Cornix

Contra potentes nemo est munitus satis;
si vero accessit conciliator maleficus,
vis et nequitia quicquid oppugnant ruit.
Aquila in sublime sustulit testudinem.
Quae cum abdidisset cornea corpus domo
nec ullo pacto laedi posset condita,
venit per auras cornix et propter volans:
"Opimam sane praedam rapuisti unguibus;
sed nisi monstraro quid sit faciendum tibi,
gravi nequiquam te lassabit pondere."
Promissa parte suadet ut scopulum super
altis ab astris duram inlidat corticem,
qua comminuta facile vescatur cibo.
Inducta vafris aquila monitis paruit,
simul et magistrae large divisit dapem.
Sic tuta quae Naturae fuerat munere,
impar duabus occidit tristi nece.

Aesop's Fables

by Phaedrus (first century)
from Latin by Terry L. Norton

The Eagle and the Crow

No one against the mighty is secure,
But might conjoined with guile none can endure.

An eagle clasped a tortoise as its prey
And soared aloft, but to his deep dismay,
No harm the sovereign lord of air could cause
Despite his razor beak and savage claws.
For in the horny aegis of his race,
The tortoise hid within his carapace.

A crow, however, flying near espied
The eagle with the plated shell and cried,
"You carry in your talons a rich prize,
Yet you will soon tire from this enterprise,
Unless you heed the tactic I advise."

"What is your scheme?" the eagle begged to know.

"But drop your burden on the rocks below,
And on the flesh you easily may feed."
The eagle acquiesced and then agreed
To share the booty should the plan succeed.

The raptor next did as the shrewd bird indicated,
The crow's advice with all speed consummated.
And he who thought that nature's gift protected
Succumbed to might by wicked guile directed.

Fables of Aesop, Book II, Fable 6

Aesop on the Success of the Wicked

A vicious dog attacked a man
And tore deep lacerations.
So he applied bread to his wounds
And sopped up blood oblations.

He tossed these gifts out to the dog
To keep in check the cur,
For he had heard such offerings
The fierce beast would deter.

On viewing what had just transpired,
Said Aesop to the man,
"Do not allow more dogs to see
Your pacifying plan.

"For if a sop holds them at bay,
Lest they eat us alive,
They'll ever want our precious blood
As their continuous bribe."

Fables of Aesop, Book II, Fable 3

Aesopus ad Quendam de Successu Inproborum

Laceratus quidam morsu vehementis canis,
tinctum cruore panem inmisit malefico,
audierat esse quod remedium vulneris.
Tunc sic Aesopus: "Noli coram pluribus
hoc facere canibus, ne nos vivos devorent,
cum scierint esse tale culpae praemium."
Successus inproborum plures allicit.

On the Flaws of Humans

Two knapsacks on us Jupiter has laid,
And what each holds is openly displayed.
Full of our faults, the first hangs down our back.
Replete with others' flaws, the second pack,
Suspended on our chest, before us lies,
And on this second one we fix our eyes.
We thus of our own faults are unaware
Yet on the flaws of others ever stare.

Fables of Aesop, Book IV, Fable 10

De Vitiis Hominum

Peras imposuit Iuppiter nobis duas:
propriis repletam vitiis post tergum dedit,
alienis ante pectus suspendit gravem.
Hac re videre nostra mala non possumus;
alii simul delinquunt, censores sumus.

Avondwandeling

Wij hebben ons vandaag verlaat!
    Pas bij de laatste brug
Waar 't voetpad tusschen 't gras vergaat,
    Daar keerden wij terug.

Achter ons dekt de witte damp
    De schemerende landen.
Zóo zijn wij thuis. Wij zien de lamp
    In loveren warande...

Wat gingen wij vanavond ver,
    Het werd alleen tè laat:
Nog verder dan de gouden ster
    Aan blauwe hemelstraat!

Zoo saam doen twee een korte poos
    Over een wijd gebied! ...
Nog liggen wegen eindeloos
    Voor morgen in 't verschiet! ...

O konden we eens zoo samen staan
    Aan de allerlaatste brug,
En saam en blij er overgaan—
    Wij kwamen nooit terug!

Evening Stroll

by P.C. Boutens (1870–1943), written in The Hague in 1909
from Dutch by Leo Zoutewelle

We wandered much too late today!
    Nearby the final bridge,
There where the trail just fades away
    We turned back towards our ridge.

Behind us rose a whitish fog
    Over the dusky lands.
In no time we'll be home, our dog
    Nuzzles with love our hands…

How far we went this eventide!
    Although it was too late:
Still farther than the golden guide
    That leads to heaven's gate.

These twain need but a little time
    To cover wide and far!…
Still endless roads are left to climb
    Tomorrow, on a star.

If we but could together stand
    At the end of this domain
And cross together hand in hand
    We'd never turn again!

Adiutor Laborantium

Adiutor laborantium,
Bonorum rector omnium,
Custos ad propugnaculum,
Defensorque credentium,
Exaltator humilium,
Fractor superbientum,
Gubernator fidelium,
Hostis impoenitentium,
Index cunctorum iudicum,
Castigator errantium,
Costa vita viventium,
Lumen et pater luminum,
Magna luce lucentium,
Nulli negans sperantium,
Opem atque auxilium,
Precor ut me homunculum,
Quassatum ac miserrimum,
Remigantem per tumultum
Saeculi istius infinitum
Trahat post se ad supernum
Vitae portum pulcherimum
Xristus;... infinitum
Ymnum sanctum in seculum
Zelo subtrahas hostium
Paradisi in gaudium.
Per te, Christe Ihesu,
Qui vivis at regnas

Adiutor Laborantium

by Colum Cille (521–597), from Latin by T.M. Moore

Ah! Helper of all workers and
Blessed Ruler of all good; You stand
Continuous guard throughout the land,
Defending every faithful man,
Extending lowly ones Your hand,
Frustrating those who in pride stand;
Great Ruler of the faithful and
Hosts who in sin prefer to stand;
In justice ruling every man,
Condemning sin by Your command;
Cascading light on every hand,
Light of the Father of lights, and
Magnificent throughout the land;
No one will You Your helping hand
Or strength deny, who in hope stand:
Please, Lord—though I am little and
Quail wretchedly before Your hand,
Resisting stormy tempests and
Strong tumults and temptations grand—
That Jesus may reach out His hand
Unto me, I implore—His land,
Verdant and lovely, be my land!
Yes, make my life a hymn to stand
Zealous against those You withstand.
Please grant that paradise my land
In Jesus Christ by grace may be,
Both now and in eternity.

TRANSLATOR'S NOTE: "Adiutor Laborantium" is an Irish poem attributed to Colum Cille, founder of the monastic community on Iona. The first letter of each line makes this an ABC poem, more or less. In this amplified translation, I have tried to capture the dynamics of this teaching poem, necessarily enlarging the Latin meanings of each line to accommodate rendering into English.

Die Lorelei

Ich weiß nicht, was soll es bedeuten,
Daß ich so traurig bin,
Ein Märchen aus uralten Zeiten,
Das kommt mir nicht aus dem Sinn.
Die Luft ist kühl und es dunkelt,
Und ruhig fließt der Rhein;
Der Gipfel des Berges funkelt,
Im Abendsonnenschein.

Die schönste Jungfrau sitzet
Dort oben wunderbar,
Ihr gold'nes Geschmeide blitzet,
Sie kämmt ihr goldenes Haar,
Sie kämmt es mit goldenem Kamme,
Und singt ein Lied dabei;
Das hat eine wundersame,
Gewalt'ge Melodei.

Den Schiffer im kleinen Schiffe,
Ergreift es mit wildem Weh;
Er schaut nicht die Felsenriffe,
Er schaut nur hinauf in die Höh'.
Ich glaube, die Wellen verschlingen
Am Ende Schiffer und Kahn,
Und das hat mit ihrem Singen,
Die Loreley getan.

The Lorelei

by Heinrich Heine (1797–1856)
from German by Anna Leader

I do not know what it might bode
That I should be so sad,
A fairytale from long ago
Now will not leave my head.
The air is cool and darkening
Above the quiet Rhine;
The mountaintops are sparkling
In afternoon sunshine.

The loveliest young maiden sits
So beautifully up there,
Her golden jewelry gleams and glints,
She combs her golden hair,
She combs it with a golden brush
And while she combs she sings;
The tune is both miraculous
And overpowering.

It grips the sailor in the ship
With a wild and aching woe;
His eyes are only looking up,
Not at the rocks below.
I believe that in the end the waves
Devoured ship and boy,
And that is what the Lorelei
Accomplished with her voice.

Quiet Night Pondering

by Li Bai (701–762)

from Chinese by Evan Mantyk

A bed before the bright moonlight.
Does frost below lie on these halls?
I lift my head: the moon is bright.
I lower it—my homeland calls!

靜夜思

床前明月光
疑是地上霜
舉頭望明月
低頭思故鄉

IX. RIDDLES AND SQUARE POEMS

On the Border by Herman Smorenburg, 2017,
oil on wood, 15.7 x 15.7 in. (HermanSmorenburg.com)

Riddle I.

by James A. Tweedie

A spike is there, but it's not gold,
Some forests have them, so I'm told.
They cannot cough, but can "ahem,"
And singers have an eye for them.
And when someone pokes fun at you
It's what they do that makes you blue.
A helpful hint? I told you so!
And that is all you need to know.

Riddle II.

by David Watt

My favorite pastime is to sleep,
And when awake, I barely creep.
Just like a friend who overstays,
I hang around for days and days.
My given name is quite offensive
To one whose slowness is defensive.
I favor garb of algae-green
With moths aplenty in between.

All riddles answers can be found on page 290.

Riddle III.

by Rupert Palmer

To those opposed to order new
I bade a merciful adieu.
The low and high I equalized,
No rank or station recognized.
"Revenge" cried them who summoned me,
Them too I slew for Liberty,
Like them I often rose and fell,
And helped to pave the road to Hell.
What am I?

Riddle IV.

by James B. Nicola

Every second, every day, she nears.
Upon arrival, though, she disappears—
Or, more accurately stated, moves away,
Still chased, while chaste yet, for another day.

Riddle V.

by Sheri-Ann O'Shea

I have a thousand faces
I have no face at all
Die not, but turn to many
—my thousand children bless my fall.

Riddle VI.

It Is Dying

by Thomas Newton

The Songs of Homer and the fame of Achilles had probably never reached the ear of the illiterate barbarian.
—*Edward Gibbon*, The Decline and Fall of the Roman Empire

The song of yourself he said you should sing,
And cut the shackles English bards begat,
And Freedom sounds so sweet. Let Freedom ring
Across the land and steamroll structures flat.
I shake my spear at Freedom's barbarous
And nasty mindless authors who betray
The values from the days of old. To us
The silly rules do *not* apply today.
Today the authors nearly all abort
The past. A few aspire to bring it back.
Is there a person giving life support
Alive today and willing to attack?
And twelve of us agree and bravely strive
For only two to show it *is* alive.

Riddle VII.

by Camilla Marx

I was no stranger to your waking mind
And you have felt me burn within your soul.
I bear your very thoughts, and yet you find
Though all may master me, none may control.
Surely I chart the heart of man: the joy
The love; the fear; the victory and despair.
Lavish, I praise, then fickle, I destroy;
I mend; I build; I crush beyond repair.
As empires shake and crumble, from their dust
I linger on to praise or to indict.
Though chained, repressed through ages, yet I must
Rise, undeterred, to lift the arm of right.
And though I rail against you, let me be;
You cannot hold me captive and be free.

Riddle VIII.

by Tonya McQuade

They each need fire to be born;
By some, a fire's scar is worn.
The fire's ash helps them to thrive—
Without it, they'd not be alive.
They grow quite tall as well as round;
In the Sierras they are found.
Their shallow roots spread far and wide
And link with others by their side.
The mightiest has a general's name—
As well as natural acclaim.
Beside them, one feels truly small—
It must strike awe to see one fall.

Riddle IX.

by N. Ram

Neither King nor rich I spare,
Lay to waste whole towns in days,
My impact is hard to bear.
Body's weakness I lay bare,
Attack health in unknown ways,
Neither King nor rich I spare.
On life, war I do declare,
Leave my victims in a daze,
My impact is hard to bear.
Doctors often dumbly stare,
At my ever-changing pace,
Neither King nor rich I spare.
I am mankind's worst nightmare,
For my death the whole world prays,
My impact is hard to bear.
I drive people to despair,
Their well-being I erase,
Neither King nor rich I spare,
My impact is hard to bear.

Riddle X.

by Julian D. Woodruff

I'm always in one place, and yet
I take you many places.
Let trails on paper not upset
You; put me through my paces!
My problem is, once in a while
I'm caught quite unaware
And lead you on mile after mile—
And also to despair.

Phobia Limerick Riddles
Name What Scares the Person

by Jan Darling

I.

Dear Santa—don't come to my house
I can cope with a shiny-faced spouse
But that stuff on your face
Suggests at its base
That it's probably hiding a louse.

II.

Some girls like to have lots of flings
And flirt with bright monarchs and kings,
But I harbor a fear
If I'm anywhere near
Those insects with colorful wings.

III.

There once was a man with twelve buns,
When into another he runs;
He counts them all up
But can't start to sup,
For their number is one that he shuns.

IV.

Old Sammy would mutter and splutter
When viewing a sandwich with butter
(Made of nuts that are found
When they're grown on the ground)
He'd throw it straight into the gutter.

V.

In a cave he would never be found,
For he'd suffer just from the mere sound;
With a fear that's intense,
He'd take leave of his sense
If a flapping he heard all around.

VI.

She would tremble with fear every morn
At the sound that her senses did warn,
Of the danger too near
In the reeds at the weir
Something slimy that sounds like a horn.

Three Riddles of Antiquity

by Rupert Palmer

I.

Half-man half-beast I seem to be,
A thousand years is naught to me,
For I watch kings and kingdoms die,
Who once were gods, beneath me lie;
In plundered graves they rest no more,
Yet still I stand, through plague and war.
My broken face hath robbed me not,
My majesty is ne'er forgot.
What am I?

II.

For countless years I worked the land
The unrequited farming-hand.
They scarce gave thanks for all my toil
Replacing seaside sand with soil,
So I destroyed them, every thief,
A king became, though of reign brief.

My wrath interred their wicked ways
That Men upon their lives might gaze.
What am I?

III.

I've been a quarry and a fort,
I've been a church, I've come to naught,
But ere my weary bones decayed
I witnessed death and accolade,
I drank the blood of many slaves,
I bore the warships on my waves.
Accursed, my purpose lived full measure
But I live on while pain brings pleasure.
What am I?

A Riddle

by Horus Hardtke

Skin hard as jade,
Mouth like a blade,
I'm seldom dry,
A dross lookst I,
And hard to find,
But my inside
Has hidden treasure
For woman's pleasure.

A Riddle

by Brian Douthit

Stalks of brown and amber and gold,
mighty when young, wither when old.
Bleached by the sun and watered daily,
Length may distinguish if lord or lady.

Body Part Riddle

by Connie Phillips

So astounding is this part—
A major muscle, like your heart.
And so astonishing its job,
Without it you would be a blob:
You couldn't stand or lift or bend—
You'd be a pretzel in the end.
A couch potato you would be
For life, if you don't set it free
With squats and stretches, lunges, presses—
Exercise that leaves you breathless.
Iliacus is next door,
And they both help support your core.
So, as I know you're sure to guess,
I'll give no hints under duress.
Just ask me what its name might be,
And I'll reply, "It's Greek to me!"

Answers.

Riddles (R): RI: Needle. RII: Sloth. RIII: Guillotine. RIV: Tomorrow. RV: Mirror. RVI: Shakespearean Sonnet. RVII: Words. RVIII: Sequoia Tree. RIX: Epidemic. RX: GPS.

Phobia (P): PI: Beards. PII: Butterflies. PIII: the Number Thirteen. PIV: Peanut Butter. PV: Bats. PVI: Frogs.

Antiquity (A): AI: The Sphinx. AII: Mt. Vesuvius. AIII: The Colosseum.

Miscellaneous: Hardtke: Oyster. Douthit: Hair. Phillips: Psoas/Hip Flexor.

Writing a Square Poem

by David Watt

I recently came across the following "square poem" attributed to 19th-century English writer Charles Dodgson (better known as Lewis Carroll). In this kind of nonmetered poem, each of the six lines may be read horizontally, or vertically from top to bottom. In other words, the first normal, horizontal line is re-created from the first word of each line, the second horizontal line is re-created from the second word of each line, and so on:

> I often wondered when I cursed,
> Often feared where I would be—
> Wondered where she'd yield her love,
> When I yield, so will she.
> I would her will be pitied!
> Cursed be love! She pitied me...

Out of curiosity, and the desire to tackle an unusual form, I wrote the following square poem:

Squarely Behind Me

> I saw no need to stay,
> Saw nothing good may follow on;
> No good could find me there—
> Need may find a better way.
> To follow me, better lay behind!
> Stay on there, way behind me!

The following are square poems from other SCP poets:

> No collusion, no obstruction.
> Collusion, frame-up, basis unproven.
> No basis for charges.
> Obstruction, unproven charges, vindication.

—Mark F. Stone

Take my love, my life, and take
My heart and all that's in me.
Love and hold it as your own;
My all! It begs you, own me!
Life that's as you will; heart-set,
And in your own heart, love me.
Take me! Own me! Set me free!

—James A. Tweedie

Dolls have eyes like daughters.
Have eyes like daughters they.
Eyes like daughters they pass;
Like daughters they pass away.
Daughters, they pass away, alas!

—Theresa Zappe

Shakespeare (Gets Burned) In Love

I have fought both long and hard.
Have a look; my hands stay scarred—
Fought. Look, dear one: Hold! En Garde!
Both my one-time loves now barred.
Long hands hold love's pain-ful shard,
And stay on, now full though charred:
Hard-scarred guard, barred shard, charred Bard.

—Amy Foreman

2020 Poetry Competition Winners

First Place ($1,000): Joseph Charles MacKenzie, New Mexico
"Rimini" "Song of the Rose" "Villanelle"
Second Place: James A. Tweedie, Washington state
"The Sound of Sunset" "The Oban Piper" "Glen Nevis"
Second Place: David Watt, Australia
"A Time Beyond" "A View from the Glade" "The Call of the Bush"
Second Place: Daniel Galef, New Jersey
"Proverbs for Engraving onto Imperial Monuments" "By a Poet of Two-and-Twenty"
Third Place: Mark F. Stone, Ohio
"Why Pterodactyls Make Great Pets" "Make Christmas a Verb" "How a Bill Can Succeed on The Hill"
Third Place: Anna J. Arredondo, Colorado
"The Turkey Vulture"
Third Place: Randal A. Burd, Jr., Missouri
"My Little Man" "Lost" "Forgotten"
Third Place: Sally Cook, New York
"Mama" "What Is In The Ground" "What We Have Come To"
Third Place: Mark Anthony Signorelli, New Jersey
"My Daughter Sees a Starling on the Lawn" "My Daughter Smiles in Her Sleep"
Fourth Place: Theresa Rodriguez, Pennsylvania
"Sebastian" "CCP and Falun Gong Sonnet" "Quasimodo"
Fourth Place: Landon Porter, Missouri
"Magicians of the Night" "Alter-Reality" "Harvest Sonnet"
Fourth Place: Michael Coy, Spain
"Et In Arcadia Ego" "Before I Saw Your Face"
Fourth Place: David Whippman, England
"Autumn Sonnet" "Marked Personal"
Fourth Place: David O'Neil, Indiana
"The Draughtsman's Dream" "Childhood Conjugation" "Time Enough for Sleep"
Fourth Place: Rod Walford, New Zealand
"Late for Supper" "Requiem for the U.N." "Eroticus Gratifica"

Fourth Place: Janice Canerdy, Mississippi
"Praise for Fall" "Shooting Stars" "Displaced: The Trail of Tears"

Translation

First Place ($100 Prize): Margaret Coats, California
    Three Translations of the Poetry of Jean Froissart
Second Place: Terry L. Norton, South Carolina
    Five Translations of Aesop's Fables, from Phaedrus
Third Place: Anna Leader, Washington, D.C.
    "The Lorelei" by Heinrich Heine
Third Place: Michael Coy, Ireland
    "A Poem" by Michelangelo, "The Woman Who Passed Me" by Charles Baudelaire

High School

First Place ($100 Prize): Luke Hahn, twelfth grade, home-schooled in Waupun, Wisconsin
    "Victus" "To a Murdered World"
Second Place: Erin Jeon, tenth grade, University High School, Irvine, California
    "At Twilight"
Second Place: Dania El-Ghattis, ninth grade, home-schooled in Melbourne, Australia
    "A Letter to Sir Grammar" "My Midnight Garden" "Crepuscular"
Third Place: Michael Zhao, eleventh grade, Lynbrook High School, San Jose, California
    "Moth, Angel of the Night" "Fallen Arbor"
Third Place: Sancia Milton, tenth grade, The Bishop's School, San Diego, California
    "Three Hundred Spartans" "Mother Teresa"
Third Place: James Preston Pack, eleventh grade, Killian Hill Christian School, Lilburn, Georgia
    "Rain"

Judges: Joseph S. Salemi, James Sale, Evan Mantyk

All First, Second, and Third Place poems appear in this Journal or on the Society's website
ClassicalPoets.org

Poets

Anderson, C.B. was the longtime gardener for the PBS television series *The Victory Garden*. Hundreds of his poems have appeared in scores of print and electronic journals out of North America, Great Britain, Ireland, Austria, Australia, and India. His collection *Mortal Soup and the Blue Yonder* was published in 2013 by White Violet Press, and his newest collection *Roots in the Sky, Boots on the Ground* was published by Kelsay Books in 2019.

Arredondo, Anna J. grew up in Pennsylvania, where she fell in love with poetry from a young age. After living in Mexico for six years, during which time she met and married her husband, she returned to Pennsylvania for one more decade. An engineer by education, home educator by choice, and poet by preference, she relocated in 2017 and currently resides in Westminster, Colorado, with her husband and three school-age children.

Bauer, Charlie resides in Apex, North Carolina, and is a salesman for a commercial carpet manufacturer.

Behrens, David Paul: After fifty thousand miles and five years as a hitchhiker, living on the road and streets in towns and cities across America, he followed with a career as an over-the-road dispatcher in the trucking industry. He is now retired and living in La Verne, California. (DavidPaulBehrens.com)

Bridges, Peter holds degrees from Dartmouth and Columbia and retired from the Foreign Service as ambassador to Somalia. Kent State University Press published his diplomatic memoir, *Safirka: An American Envoy*, and the biographies of John Moncure Daniel and Donn Piatt. He has self-published a volume of a hundred sonnets from the Elk Mountains and a memoir titled *Woods Waters Peaks: A Diplomat Outdoors*.

Bryant, Mike is a poet and retired plumber living on the Gulf Coast of Texas.

Bryant, Susan Jarvis is a church secretary and poet whose homeland is Kent, England. She is now an American citizen living on the coastal plains of Texas.

Burd, Jr., Randal A. is an educator, freelance editor, writer, and poet. His freelance writing includes assignments on the paid writing team for Ancestry.com and multiple online blogs, newsletters, and publications. Randal received his master's degree in English curriculum and instruction from the University of Missouri. He currently works on the site of a residential treatment facility for juveniles in rural Missouri. He lives in southeast Missouri with his wife and two children.

Canerdy, Janice is a retired high-school English teacher from Potts Camp, Mississippi. Her first book, *Expressions of Faith* (Christian Faith Publishing), was published in December 2016.

Carlson, Donald lives and works in North Central Texas. In 2015, he collaborated on a volume of poetry with two friends and fellow poets, Timothy Donohue and Dennis Patrick Slattery. Their joint collection, *Road Frame Window*, was published by Mandorla Press. In addition, he recently published a collection of verse titled *Testimony: A Poetic Retelling of the Gospel According to John* independently.

Carter, Jared is a poet living in Indiana. His most recent book of poems is *The Land Itself*, from Monongahela Books in West Virginia.

Coats, Margaret lives in California. She holds a Ph.D. in English and American literature and language from Harvard University. She has retired from a career of teaching literature, languages, and writing that included considerable work in home-schooling for her own family and others.

Cook, Sally is a former Wilbur Fellow and six-time Pushcart nominee. She is a regular contributor to *National Review*, and has appeared in various venues, including *Trinacria*. Also a painter, her present works in the style known as Magic Realism are represented in national collections such as the NSDAR Museum in Washington, D.C., and the Burchfield Penney Art Center in Buffalo, New York.

Coy, Michael, a barrister, teacher, and journalist, is an Irish poet who has settled permanently in the south of Spain. He readily admits to a serious rhyme-and-rhythm habit. He is winner of various poetry prizes in Britain and Ireland.

Crisell, Rob is a writer, actor, teacher, and attorney in Temecula, California. After two decades in publishing, national nonprofit work, law, and commercial real estate, he's now a full-time writer, actor, and educator. He is an outside instructor with the Murrieta Valley Union School District, where he teaches poetry and Shakespeare. He also teaches at the St. Jeanne de Lestonnac School and other area schools on behalf of Shakespeare in the Vines (SITV). He runs SITV's annual high school monologue competition, which he began in 2013. He's the author/actor of *Red, White & Bard! A Celebration of Shakespeare in America* and *Hamlet's Guide to Happiness: 7 Life Lessons from the Greatest Play Ever Written*, one-man shows he has performed for SITV, schools, and the Osher Lifelong Learning Institute. He lives in Temecula with his wife and their two children.

Curtis, Michael, an architect, sculptor, painter, historian, and poet, has for more than forty years contributed to the revival of the classical arts. He has taught and lectured at universities, colleges, and museums, including The Institute of Classical Architecture, The National Gallery of Art, et cetera; his pictures and statues are housed in over four hundred private and public collections, including The Library of Congress, The Supreme Court, et alibi; his verse has been published in over twenty journals; his work in the visual arts can be found at TheClassicalArtist.com, and his literary work can be found at TheStudioBooks.com.

Damigo, Tony L. is contributing poet and participant at local "Open Mic" readings in the Crestview, Florida, area. He is also a poet of the Society of Creative Anachronism, a Renaissance reenactment organization.

Darling, Jan is a New Zealander who has worked in Auckland, Wellington, London, Barcelona, New York, and Sydney at copywriting and marketing strategy. She has spent her leisure time over sixty years writing poetry and short stories. Now retired, she lives in pastoral New South Wales with her husband, Arturo.

Douthit, Brian is a full-time Ph.D. Student at Duke University School of Nursing in Durham, North Carolina.

El-Ghattis, Dania is a grade nine home-schooled student in Melbourne, Australia.

Elster, Martin serves as a percussionist with the Hartford Symphony Orchestra. His poems have appeared in numerous journals and anthologies. Honors include co-winner of RhymeZone's 2016 poetry contest, winner of the Thomas Gray Anniversary Poetry Competition 2014, third place in the Science Fiction Poetry Association's 2015 poetry contest, and three Pushcart nominations.

Foreman, Amy hails from the southern Arizona desert, where she homesteads with her husband and seven children. She has enjoyed teaching both English and music at the college level, but is now focused on home-schooling her children, gardening, farming, and writing. Recently, she has launched a blog of her poetry, *The Occasional Caesura: A Pause Midline* (TheOccasionalCaesura.WordPress.com)

Fuller, Annabelle reads classics and English at Magdalen College, Oxford, where she is a member of the Florio Society. She won the Forward Young Critics Prize in 2017 and the BBC Proms Poetry Competition in 2018.

Galef, Daniel: His comic verse has been widely published, and he is a featured author in the *Potcake Chapbooks* series of mini-anthologies from Sampson Low.

Galef, David has published over two hundred poems in a wide range of magazines. He's also published two poetry volumes, *Flaws* and *Kanji Poems*, as well as two chapbooks, *Lists* and *Apocalypses*. Unable to stop himself, he's also written fiction, literary essays, and translation, over a dozen books in all. In real life, he directs the creative writing program at Montclair State University. (DavidGalef.com)

Gallucci, Raymond is a retired professional engineer who has been writing poetry since 1990.

Glassman, Michael is a retired social studies teacher living in Newburgh, New York. He is seventy-five years old.

Glyn-Jones, William, currently working in marketing, studied English and media and then got a master's degree in the history of art. A longtime lover of the classical tradition, he lived in Greece for a time teaching English, but now lives in a cottage outside the city of Bath in the United Kingdom with his wife, two young daughters, and a voracious guinea pig.

Graham, J. David is a father, husband, and poet. He is a classicist by training, currently working on a metered translation of the *Aeneid*.

Grein, Dusty is a poet, novelist, editor, and book producer. His written work has been published in numerous magazines and books, as well as in print and online journals. He self-published his first novel, *The Sleeping Giant* in 2015, and his first poetry book, *a mist shrouded path*, was published in 2019 by RhetAskew Publishing. He has had poetry translated into several languages worldwide, is the co-author of a book on crafting classical poetry, and his How To articles can be found reprinted in several locations. Dusty lives, works, and plays in the Pacific Northwestern United States, where he enjoys spending time whenever possible spoiling many of his fourteen grandchildren, before sending them back home to their parents.

Hahn, Luke is a twelfth-grade student home-schooled in Waupun, Wisconsin.

Hardtke, Horus is currently a full-time student at St. Louis University in Missouri, majoring in psychology with a minor in theology.

Hartley, Peter is a retired painting restorer. He was born in Liverpool and lives in Manchester, U.K. His book, *On a Boat to Barra*, was published in 2019.

Hay, C. David is a retired dentist living in Indiana and Florida. He received his B.S. and Doctor of Dental Surgery degrees from Indiana University. He is the author of five books of poetry, which are dedicated to his wife, Joy. He has been widely published nationally and abroad, and his poetry has been read on the British Broadcasting Channel. He has been nominated for the Pushcart Prize in Poetry and is the recipient of the Ordo Honoris Award from Kappa Delta Rho.

Hayes, Edward C. "Ted" was a university faculty member (Ph.D. in political science from the University of California, 1967) and freelancer in his early career. He moved into full-time journalism and is now retired.

Hodges, Ron L. is an English teacher and poet who lives in Orange County, California. He won First Place in the Society of Classical Poets 2016 Poetry Competition.

Hoke, Edward studies acting and classics at Northwestern University. (For weekly poetry-based posts and photos, follow on Instagram at @blandmagyar)

Jeon, Erin is a tenth-grade student at University High School in Irvine, California.

Keefe, Philip was born in Wales and educated in England. A sometime carpenter, sailor, and song lyricist, he is now a naturalized American citizen retired and living in Rockledge, Florida.

Kelly, Conor was born in Dublin and spent his adult life teaching in a school in the Dublin suburbs. He now lives in a rural area of West Clare in Ireland, from where he manages his Twitter site, @poemtoday, dedicated to the short poem. He has had poems printed in Irish, British, American, and Mexican magazines. He was shortlisted for a Hennessy New Irish Writers award.

Lauretta, M.P. lives in the U.K., where she enjoys watching (and writing about) nature and current events. She is currently working on two new collections: one of sonnets and one of villanelles. Her first collection, *To a Blank Page and Other Poems*, is still available from Amazon, Apple iBooks, and Barnes & Noble.

Leach, Daniel R. is a poet living in Houston, Texas. He has spent much of his life fighting for the ideals of classical culture and poetry. His volume of poetry, compiling over twenty years of composition, is titled *Voices on the Wind*.

Leader, Anna: Born to American and British parents and raised in Luxembourg, she graduated from Princeton University in 2018 and now works in an education noprofit in Washington, D.C. In addition to literary translations, Anna writes poetry, plays, and novels. She has twice been awarded the Stephen Spender Prize for Poetry in Translation (2013 and 2015, under-18 category), and most recently won the 2019 Harvill Secker Young Translators' Prize, administered by Penguin Random House, for a prose translation from the original French.

Lukey, Benjamin Daniel was born in 1986. He has lived all over the Eastern United States and currently resides near Charlotte, North Carolina. He teaches high school English classes whenever he is not fishing or writing poetry.

MacKenzie, Joseph Charles is a traditional lyric poet and the only American to have won the Scottish International Poetry Competition. He has been nominated for the Pushcart Prize. His book, *Sonnets for Christ the King*, was published by MCP Books in 2018. (MacKenziePoet.com)

Magdalen, Daniel is a doctoral student in the Faculty of Letters at the University of Bucharest, in Romania.

Maibach, Michael Charles began writing poems at age nine. Since then, he has continued writing poems and sharing them with friends. His career has involved global business diplomacy. He is a native of Peoria, Illinois. Today Michael resides in Old Town, Alexandria, Virginia.

Mantyk, Evan teaches history and literature in the Hudson Valley region of New York, where he lives with his wife and two children. He is president of The Society of Classical Poets, as well as chief editor of its website and journal. His most recent book of poetry, *Heroes of the East and West*, was published by Classical Poets Publishing in 2020.

Martin, Lynn Michael lives in Hagerstown, Maryland. He edits the *Curator*, a poetry publication, and loves to read Middle English literature.

Marx, Camilla lives with her husband, Bryan, in Grahamstown, South Africa. She completed a B.A. Theology (Hons) in historical theology, and in her spare time enjoys reading, opera, history, and walking.

McKee, Nathaniel Todd: His interest in classical poetry first grew while studying for a master's in business administration at the University of Oxford, U.K. Somehow this whimsical place deepened an already strong appreciation for the humanities, even as he studied business. Nathaniel's literary interests include Greek and Roman classics, 18th– and 19th-century English and French literature, the Bible, and history in general. He currently purchases agricultural commodities and energy for a mid-sized food manufacturing company in the foothills of southeastern Tennessee, where he lives with his wife, Bethany.

McQuade, Tonya is an English teacher at Los Gatos High School in Los Gatos, California, and lives with her husband in San Jose, California. She has been writing poetry since fourth grade and is currently a member of Poetry Center San Jose.

Milton, Sancia is a tenth-grade student at The Bishop's School in San Diego.

Moore, T.M. and his wife, Susie, make their home in the Champlain Valley of Vermont. He is principal of The Fellowship of Ailbe, and the author of eight books of poetry. He and Susie have collaborated on more than thirty books, which may be found, together with their many other writings and resources, including the daily teaching letter *Scriptorium*, at Ailbe.org.

Newton, Thomas is an electronics engineer and poet living in Winter Springs, Florida.

Nicholson, Jeff is a lifelong poet with a particular affinity for writing formal verse. He currently resides in rural Clark County, outside Battle Ground, Washington, with his wife and a few lingering adult children. Though his educational background is in English and theology, Jeff currently directs the technical services department for a global architectural glass coatings manufacturer in Ridgefield, Washington.

Nicola, James B. is a writer whose nonfiction book *Playing the Audience* won a Choice award. His two poetry collections, published by Word Poetry, are *Manhattan Plaza* (2014) and *Stage to Page: Poems from the Theater* (2016). He won a Dana Literary Award, a People's Choice award (from *Storyteller* magazine), and a *Willow Review* award; was nominated twice for a Pushcart Prize and once for a Rhysling Award; and was featured poet in *The New Formalist*.

Norton, Terry L. is professor emeritus of literacy at Winthrop University in Rock Hill, South Carolina, and is the author of *Cherokee Myths and Legends*. He is a longtime student of French, Spanish, and Latin.

Oratofsky, Paul was born in Brooklyn, New York, in 1943 and has been writing poems since 1954. He recently self-published his first book—a collection of related poetic works called *Continuum*. His website, Oratofsky.com, shows a sampling of his artwork and history. He studied poetry for eight and a half years with the poet José Garcia Villa, starting in 1968.

Ortiz, Martin Hill is a researcher and professor at the Ponce University of Health Sciences in Ponce, Puerto Rico, where he lives with his wife and son. He has three novels published by small presses: *A Predatory Mind* (Loose Leaves Publishing, 2013), *Never Kill a Friend* (Ransom Note Press, 2015), and *A Predator's Game* (Rook's Page, 2016).

O'Shea, Sheri-Ann is a South African-born teacher now living in Brisbane, Australia, with her husband and three lively boys.

Pack, James Preston is an eleventh grader at Killian Hill Christian School in Lilburn, Georgia.

Palmer, Rupert, born 1988, lives in Benoni, South Africa, where he is a consultant in the mining industry by trade.

Pearman, Jared is a writer and producer in Calgary, Canada.

Peterson, Roy E. is an author, former diplomat, and retired U.S. Army Military Intelligence and Russian Foreign Area Officer who currently resides in Texas.

Phillips, Connie is a former English teacher and editor living in Massachusetts.

Porter, Landon is an entrepreneur and database developer in Kansas City, Missouri, where he lives with his wife and three children.

Ram, N. is a poet living in Mumbai, India.

Ream, Alexander King is a poet living in Tennessee. A member of the Demosthenian Literary Society at the University of Georgia, he deployed to Hawija, then wrote on Lookout Mountain, continuing with Delta Kappa Epsilon International. Berkeley, Ann Arbor, and Athens encouraged him as a writer.

Rizley, Martin grew up in Oklahoma and in Texas, and has served in pastoral ministry both in the United States and in Europe. He is currently serving as the pastor of a small evangelical church in the city of Málaga on the southern coast of Spain, where he lives with his wife and daughter. Martin has enjoyed writing and reading poetry as a hobby since his early youth.

Robin, Damian lives in England, where he works as a copyeditor and proofreader. He lives with his wife and two of their three adult children. He won Second Place in the Society's 2014 Poetry Competition.

Rodriguez, Ramón, LC, is a religious brother studying for the priesthood. He lives in Rome, where he studies philosophy at the Pontifical Atheneum Regina Aposolorum.

Rodriguez, Theresa is the author of *Jesus and Eros: Sonnets, Poems and Songs*, a chapbook of thirty-seven sonnets, and *Longer Thoughts* (Shanti Arts, 2020). She is a retired classical singer and voice teacher who has written for *Classical Singer* magazine. She recently released an album titled *Lullabies: Traditional American and International Songs*, which is available on all streaming services.

Sale, James, is a leading expert on motivation, and the creator and licensor of Motivational Maps worldwide. James has been writing poetry for over forty years and has seven collections of poems published, including most recently *Inside the Whale*, his metaphor for being in a hospital and surviving cancer, which afflicted him in 2011. He can be found at the website JamesSale.Co.uk and contacted at james@motivationalmaps.com. He is the winner of First Prize in the Society's 2017 Competition and Second Prize in the Society's 2015 Competition.

Salemi, Joseph S. has published five books of poetry, and his poems, translations, and scholarly articles have appeared in over one hundred publications worldwide. He is the editor of the literary magazine *Trinacria*. He teaches in the Department of Humanities at New York University and in the Department of Classical Languages at Hunter College.

Sarangi, Satyananda, an electrical engineering alumnus of Indira Gandhi Institute of Technology, is a young poet and editor who enjoys reading Longfellow, Shelley, Coleridge, Yeats, Blake, and many others. His works have been widely published in India, Germany, and the United States, among other countries. Currently, he resides in Odisha, India.

Sedia, Adam (born in 1984) lives in his native Northwest Indiana with his wife, Ivana, and their children; he practices law as a civil and appellate litigator. He is also a composer, and his musical works may be heard on his YouTube channel.

Signorelli, Mark Anthony is a poet and author whose work has appeared in a variety of journals. He is a member of the Academy of Philosophy and Letters.

Stock, Beverly is an emerging poet and a retired communications manager. She has published feature articles in magazines and newspapers in five countries. Beverly divides her time between St. Louis, Missouri; and Santa Fe, New Mexico.

Stone, Mark F. grew up near Seattle, Washington. After graduating from Brandeis University and Stanford Law School, he worked as an attorney for the United States Air Force for thirty-three years. He served eleven years as an active duty Air Force JAG attorney. He then served twenty-two years as an Air Force civilian attorney (while serving part time in the Air Force Reserves as a JAG attorney). He began writing poems in 2005, as a way to woo his bride-to-be into wedlock. He recently retired, giving him time to focus on poetry. He lives in central Ohio.

Sugar, Alan shares his poetry and performance art in Decatur, Georgia, where he currently resides. He is also a puppeteer, and he has worked as a special education teacher in the public schools of Atlanta. Currently, Alan works as a writing tutor at Georgia State University Perimeter College, Clarkston Campus.

Sunderam, Rohini is a Canadian of Indian origin. She is a semi-retired advertising copywriter whose articles and stories have appeared in India and Canada. As Zohra Saeed, she is the author of *Desert Flower* (Ex-L-Ence Publishing, U.K.). She was a contributor to the anthologies *My Beautiful Bahrain* (Miracle Publishing, Bahrain), *More of My Beautiful Bahrain*, and *Poetic Bahrain* (Robin Barratt Publishing, U.K.), and *Corpoetry*—a collection of poems satirizing corporate life (Ex-L-Ence Publishing).

Tessitore, Joe is a retired New York City resident and poet.

Tweedie, James A. is a retired pastor living in Long Beach, Washington. He likes to walk on the beach with his wife. He has written and self-published four novels and a collection of short stories.

Van Inman, Clinton was born in Walton-on-Thames, England, in 1945. He graduated from San Diego State University in 1977 and is now a retired high school English teacher in Tampa Bay, Florida, where he lives with his wife, Elba.

Venable, Peter has been writing poetry for fifty years. He has been published widely and is a member of the Winston Salem Writers.

Villanueva, Angel L. is a religious man who resides in Massachusetts, enjoying a simple life with his lovely wife, Nina.

Walford, Rod is an Englishman living in Auckland, New Zealand, and has been writing poetry for some twenty-five years. He is a semi-retired diesel fuel injection engineer. He has self-published several books of rhyming poetry, including *Timeless*, *Real Poetry for Real Women (written by a man)*, and *One Hour before the Dawn*. (RodWalfordPoetry.com)

Watt, David is a writer from Canberra, the "Bush Capital" of Australia. When not working for IP (Intellectual Property) Australia, he finds time to appreciate the intrinsic beauty of traditional rhyming poetry. He was the First Place winner in the Friends of Falun Gong Poetry Contest 2018.

Whippman, David is a British poet, now retired after a career in healthcare. Over the years he's had quite a few poems, articles, and short stories published in various magazines.

Williams, Ian is a thirty-year-old resident of Halifax, Nova Scotia, Canada.

Winebrenner, Caleb is a storyteller, poet, and educator whose mission in life is to guide our discovery of our lost humanity (including the traditions of humanities in the West). He holds a B.A. in linguistics, an M.A. in educational theater, and a certificate in transformative language arts.

Wise, Bruce Dale (aka BDW) is a poet living in Texas who often writes under anagrammatic heteronyms. He won First Prize in the Society of Classical Poets' 2014 Competition.

Woodruff, Julian D. was a teacher, orchestral musician, and librarian. He served for several years as librarian at the Crocker Art Museum in Sacramento, California. He now resides in the area of Rochester, New York, where he writes poetry and fiction, much of it for children.

Wyler, E.V. "Beth" is a poet and writer living in New Jersey.

Yankevich, Leo was a poet who was born in Pennsylvania and lived in Poland. His latest books are *The Last Silesian* (The Mandrake Press, 2005), *Tikkun Olam & Other Poems* (Second Expanded Edition; Counter-Currents Publishing, 2012), and *Journey Late at Night: Poems & Translations* (Counter-Currents Publishing, 2013). He was editor of *The New Formalist*. More of his work can be found at LeoYankevich.com. He passed away in December 2018.

Zappe, Theresa was once a high school Spanish teacher and is now a home educator in New York. She and her husband are much occupied with math, meals, science, soccer games, sentence diagrams, dirty dishes, Latin, and laundry.

Zavlanov, Gleb is a young poet and songwriter living in New York City. He is a 2017 graduate of Townsend Harris High School.

Zhao, Michael is an eleventh-grade student at Lynbrook High School in San Jose, California.

Zoutewelle, Leo was born in 1935 in the Netherlands and was raised there until at age twenty he immigrated to the United States. He received his Bachelor of Science degree in mathematics from Davidson College, in North Carolina, and a master's in business administration from the Darden School at the University of Virginia. In 1977, he went into business for himself in the field of land surveying, which he maintained until 2012, when he retired. Since then, he has written an autobiography and two novels (unpublished).

RHETASKEW PUBLISHING

www.ingramcontent.com/pod-product-compliance
Lightning Source LLC
Chambersburg PA
CBHW050312120526
44592CB00014B/1880